Ego at the Helm

The Hidden Cost of
Narcissism in Leadership

Robert A. Damon

Ego at the Helm: The Hidden Cost of Narcissism in Leadership

Copyright © 2025 by Robert A. Damon and Great Ridge Group LLC

All rights reserved, including the right of reproduction in whole or in part in any form without prior permission of the publisher, except as provided by USA copyright law.

Scripture taken from the HOLY BIBLE, NEW INTERNATIONAL VERSION ® Copyright © 1973, 1978, 1984 by International Bible Society. Used by permission of Zondervan. All rights reserved.

The "NIV" and "New International Version" trademarks are registered in the United States Patent and Trademark Office by International Bible Society. Use of either trademark requires the permission of International Bible Society.

Published by Great Ridge Group LLC
Saint Paul, Minnesota, USA
www.GreatRidge.com

Additional media available at www.GreatRidge.com.
For more information or to contact the author, please visit www.GreatRidge.com.

Cover design: Terry Dugan
Cover image credit: slowbuzzstudio@Adobe Stock
Editorial team: Scott Noble and Cristina Wright
Interior layout: Ben Wolf, Inc.

ISBN-13 (hardcover): 979-8-9936936-0-6
ISBN-13 (softcover): 979-8-9936936-1-3
ISBN-13 (eBook): 979-8-9936936-2-0

First Printing, 2025

Printed in the United States of America

CONTENTS

Foreword	v
Introduction	ix
My Story: The Lead-Up	1
1. Understanding Narcissism	5
My Story: The Point of Crisis	15
2. Narcissism In Christian Leadership	23
3. Subsequent Truths	29
4. Abuse, Hubris, And Power	35
My Story: Processing What Happened	43
5. Tools for Prevention	47
My Story: What We Did	55
6. In The Midst Of The Fight	63
My Story: The Epilogue	81
7. Recommended Plan of Action	85
Appendix A: Tools, in Detail	89
Appendix B: Code of Conduct	99
Appendix C: A Few Words on Forgiveness	105
Bibliography	107
Acknowledgments	113
About the Author	115

FOREWORD

If you work *with* or *for* a narcissist, you have quite a journey ahead. You probably know that already.

In *Ego at the Helm*, my friend Robert Damon pulls back the curtain just a little bit into an extraordinarily painful season that he endured and shares lessons he has learned. You might well find yourself reading this book with a specific person (or two) in mind, nodding and feeling like you might have language now to describe what you're going through.

The narcissistic leader is all too familiar to many of us. They demand loyalty but only offer it to suppliants and unquestioning supporters. They need to be the biggest person in the room—experts in both self-aggrandizement and the capacity to subtly put others in their place. They dominate discussions and believe themselves to have impeccable judgment and unfailing capacity. They need nobody's counsel. They want nobody's guidance. They never fail, but, in their minds, suffer by association with lesser individuals. They can be superficially warm and endearing for a time, but lack patience and empathy for those who fail to provide sufficient affirmation. They create their own rules and feel entitled to perks and power that might not have been theirs originally. They can be great on the platform but poor interpersonally.

You've likely met men and women like this, and that's why you picked up this book.

In the pages that follow, Robert Damon paints a compelling and disturbing picture of a narcissist ("Keith") who wounded countless people, including his own family. Robert's description of the events will leave you a little breathless, but the story is not just about identifying the danger but also dealing with the destructive aftermath.

Narcissists won't read this book. It's a mirror into which they will not look. But to all of us who have been pushed out by a narcissist, or who are trying to outlast a narcissist, there are vital nuggets of encouragement, hope, and wisdom throughout this book.

Narcissism is not a condition with tight parameters. It's more of a spectrum, ranging from benevolent narcissists whose leadership helps but also limits the growth of a church or organization, to much more aggressive and sophisticated narcissists whose leadership eventually threatens to bring down the entire organization. Some narcissists seem to be excessively prideful; others slip into deeply hurtful, manipulative, and even abusive behavior. Some will gently tighten their grip on power and authority; others will wage all-out war for it. Whomever you might have encountered in the past, or find yourself currently serving, Robert has gathered some helpful research on narcissism and put it at your fingertips.

This is a book about people and personalities. It is also a book about building culture and building our own lives (self-leadership). I'm encouraged by Robert's wisdom and his willingness to share out of his own pain and conflict. We can learn from each other. We certainly can learn from him.

Christian leadership is too often oversimplified. We bring

to our kingdom assignments a sense of call from God, hope for the future, willingness to work hard, faith in the leading of the Holy Spirit, and commitment to Christ. We also bring our brokenness from the past, our woundedness from childhood, and our "disordered desires" (to quote Augustine). And we bring all of our personal complexity and seek to lead communities with their own immense intricacies and convolutions.

Robert does not ignore these complexities, but he does exhort us to establish boundaries, relationships, policies, and practices that will best serve not only us but those whom we lead. Read through these insights thoughtfully and prayerfully. Integrate these principles into your life as much as possible.

While the Holy Spirit continues His good work of sanctification within each of us, we can partner with Him by taking practical steps to guard our hearts, minds, relationships, and workplaces for the glory of God and the cause of His kingdom in the world.

I commend this book to you.

David Timms, PhD
Dean, School of Theology & Leadership
Dean, Multnomah Biblical Seminary
Director, Center for Church Health
Jessup University, Rocklin, CA
October 2025

Dr. Timms has authored several books on life and leadership:

- *Just Leave God Out of It! The Cultural Compromises Christians Make*
- *Sacred Waiting: Waiting on God in a World that Waits for Nothing*
- *The Power of Blessing: How a Carefully Chosen Word Changes Everything*
- *Living the Lord's Prayer*
- *Reflections through Romans: A Lenten Devotional*
- *Shape Your World: Transformational Leadership for Everyday Life*
- *40 Days in Israel: A Spiritual Pilgrimage*
- *Choosing Hospitality over Hostility*
- *A Thoughtful Gospel: Living Out God's Story Today*
- *Before You Walk Away: When Violence, Vengeance, Anger, or Apathy of God Drives You to the Brink*
- *Exhausted: Thirty Days to Rethink and Rediscover Rest*

Titles are available on Amazon.

INTRODUCTION

Narcissism is a growing issue for organizations, especially when leadership roles require visible trust and interaction with the community to achieve mission success.

Multiple resources and research available over the past forty years define common traits and concerns about narcissistic behaviors in leadership. However, understanding the issue of narcissism in leadership is one thing, but recognizing key indicators and developing best practices to manage it is becoming infinitely more challenging, especially when most people do not feel the need to learn about it until it is already a problem.

This is particularly challenging when narcissistic leaders initially seem effective and driven, even exceptionally talented, like the heroes of the organization, until their egos and manipulation create abusive chaos and a trail of emotional and spiritual debris.

I hope the following definitions and recommendations will help you and your organization understand the potential negative impacts of narcissistic leadership—professionally and personally. With this book, I encourage organizations, leaders, emerging leaders, family, and friends to recognize and respond to narcissistic behaviors before they become community-wide concerns.

Shortly after accepting a new role as associate pastor in a growing Midwest suburban congregation, I was introduced to a local Christian counselor. When we mentioned a mutual acquaintance, he said, "Does he have any idea how arrogant he comes across?" In that discussion, I was encouraged to learn everything I could about narcissism.

Little did I know that I would not only learn about narcissism but also face down narcissistic leaders in several organizational settings. In the past several decades, I have encountered many people who have either significantly hampered the organizations they served or experienced personal and professional failure as a direct result of narcissistic tendencies left unchecked.

In one case, the narcissistic leader was emotionally abusing staff over several years and creating a complicated financial accounting system within the organization's bookkeeping. This gave her an increase in compensation without notice, resulting in her pocketing additional funds through falsified records.

In another situation, the narcissistic leader was supervising a satellite site of a nonprofit community group and operating without regard for consequences to the organization. It was his right, he said; the organization would be nothing without him, he said. Confronting these behaviors created huge issues for the organization and the local community he served. The constituents reacted strongly to his reprimand and eventual employment separation. But things settled down quickly, and now the organization is stronger than ever.

In yet another experience, a visibly narcissistic leader had a horrific character and moral failure with multiple sexual engagements over several years—as well as a brutal home life—

which ended his career, marriage, and many of his personal and professional relationships.

And in another setting, a man was behaving in narcissistic ways, but he was not someone who would be classified as a narcissist. His mental status could be described as obsessive-compulsive, abusive, and even psychotic, but the presenting behaviors were strongly narcissistic in nature. Working in a nonprofit organization, this leader had a profound impact.

The following research and recommendations are a result of my efforts to come to grips with the reality of narcissism in leadership, especially focused on nonprofit or faith-based organizations. This is not meant to be an academic study or diagnostic tool; there are plenty of those already published. I wish to define patterns of behavior, ways to recognize these patterns quickly in ourselves and others, and identify what systems leaders and organizations can develop to avoid nurturing narcissistic behaviors.

I hope the research and recommendations assist nonprofits and faith-based organizations to take the question of accountability and narcissistic behavior seriously and to use various tools to allow organizations to focus on people and the organization's mission.

I am not a psychologist or psychiatric professional. I am an experienced pastoral counselor and organizational leader who is blessed to be surrounded by some of the best professionals who have shared so much with me over decades of interaction.

This book began as reading notations, quickly morphed into a working paper, then a white paper, and finally into the book you are now reading. My apologies if any references are lacking, incorrect, or missing.

Yes, I have been negatively impacted by narcissistic abusers. The journey from "That wouldn't happen here" to "Oh my, what just happened?" has been a turbulent road of awareness and remorse. For those who suffered when I didn't see or figure out what was going on until it was too late, I offer my deepest apologies.

In my situation, while both my own and the organization's actions were imperfect, we tried to do the right things. Hindsight is always clear, and self-proclaimed and vocal armchair experts, or pseudo-psychologists' pronouncements, are rarely fair in tone or measured with significant perspective.

The words "woulda," "coulda," and "shoulda" have seasoned my thinking. But this truth is clear: narcissistic behavior has life-shattering consequences and can happen anywhere, to anyone, at any time, regardless of education, appearance, setting, experience, personality, intentions, and words of promise.

J. R. R. Tolkien writes in *The Two Towers*: "We shouldn't be here at all, if we'd known more about it before we started. But I suppose it's often that way ... Folk seem to have been just landed in them, usually—their paths were laid that way, as you put it. But I expect they had lots of chances, like us, of turning back, only they didn't . . . I wonder what sort of tale we have fallen into."[1]

Robert A. Damon
Saint Paul, Minnesota
October 2025

---

1. J. R. R. Tolkien, *The Two Towers* (London: HarperCollins, 2005), 301-302.

MY STORY: THE LEAD-UP

"Leadership of any sort can be a challenging endeavor and Christian leadership sets some of the highest standards of morality for those in positions of power and influence."
—J. Kwabena Asamoah-Gyadu

Throughout this book, I will share my story alongside the information gathered. I'm sharing my story as a personal reflection of events, and I hope it may be a helpful reference point for the research. The narrative is not meant to be an exact or detailed account. I've changed—or altogether omitted—names to honor confidentiality.

My wife and I started attending a suburban congregation of 1,200 people when I was working at a local college, and we sought a church community to call home.

The first Sunday at this church, we were impressed by the quality of the worship service, excellent use of scripture, friendly feel of the congregation, and the deep scriptural preaching. We met the senior pastor and found him to be a bit eccentric but likable, and we determined to make this our place of worship and service.

Within weeks, we found peace and spiritual growth because of the people, studies, worship, and overall sense of mission. We also became aware that the senior pastor (Keith, as we will call him in this narrative) was dominant, and at times even seemed arrogant, but his teaching and biblical knowledge were exceptional.

My wife and I became involved with teaching and prayer, and our natural tendency for caregiving was part of our attitude toward community. We felt this was a place we could be for a long time, Lord willing.

After several years as active members of the congregation, I was approached by the then-executive pastor and senior pastor Keith to consider leaving my role in a para-church ministry and joining the staff as an associate pastor. It was not a difficult decision, and God seemed to be leading us into a new season and back into local church ministry. I agreed to join the staff.

I grew closer to the congregation, the staff, and Keith, who was now my boss. Being present every day with the staff and leadership, I saw firsthand Keith's dominance and arrogance, but it was moderated by his good preaching and the peacekeeping efforts of staff and elders. There seemed to be more good things than bad.

The congregation was thriving with a lot of people coming into the community and finding spiritual growth. There were weddings, funerals, events, and activities, and it seemed like a functional family.

People were coming and going as part of the community, but that can be normal in a larger congregation. We did see a moderately high turnover in staff and leadership, but in an environment of gifted people, this is not terribly uncommon. There was a growing distance between staff and elders, but many of those challenges were attributed to the rapid growth of the congregation. At least, that's what we thought.

Personally, the preaching and quality worship were drawing me closer to God. I was learning more in my faith, and my spiritual journey was strong. It seemed like the perfect place to serve. At least, that's what I thought.

I eventually moved from my role as pastor of shepherding to pastor of adult ministry and finally, to executive pastor.

My role as executive pastor was putting my decades of ministry experience to good use, and I felt fulfilled. It seemed like my gifts and personality were helpful to the congregation and to leadership. Some said I was a good balance to Keith's sometimes aggressive behavior, that I was a calming influence and provided boundaries for staff and leadership, which was especially helpful considering Keith's chaotic leadership style.

It was hard but rewarding work, and it required long days and many difficult conversations to moderate Keith's weird behavior. He would often change decisions or plans, and we had to pay close attention to what he did or said.

However, God seemed to be working in the life of this community, and we felt a vitality and energy in what we were doing.

Yet, we saw a growing negative energy in Keith. He was demanding, often angry about this or that, and complained about anything or anyone that seemed at odds with his thoughts or plans. He would be absent from meetings or the office, showing up at odd times and leaving abruptly. Leadership complained about Keith in private—and at times, even in meetings. He seemed to be driving people away, both church members and leadership, rather than drawing them into a peaceful place of community and spiritual growth.

Something was happening, but no one could discern what was wrong, and Keith dismissed any attempts to discover the cause.

Keith seemed to rally around those people who agreed with his thinking and those who would applaud his efforts, and he would demean or distance himself from anyone who did not. Staff and elders who did not agree with Keith were driven away, and congregation members who did not give in to his thinking were encouraged to go elsewhere. Keith bad-mouthed me to others privately, and sometimes even in front of leadership and staff during meetings.

While the community was good and my role fulfilling, moderating Keith's behavior and doing my job were becoming almost impossible.

> *"No matter how much you beg a narcissist to stop, they will push you past your limits until you snap, then when you do, they'll stand back and act shocked, play the victim and claim you're crazy."*
> —Lana Horowitz

> *"... Sin is crouching at your door;*
> *it desires to have you, but you must rule over it."*
> —Genesis 4:7, NIV

Worldmetrics.org reports (2025)

- 45% of victims of religious abuse reported experiencing emotional manipulation or control
- 80% of religious abuse victims felt betrayed by their faith leaders
- 65% of religious abuse victims report that their trust in religious institutions is permanently damaged

CHAPTER ONE
UNDERSTANDING NARCISSISM

> *"A shepherd who is not first a lamb is a dangerous shepherd and has ceased to follow the Good Shepherd. Our primary identity in life, if we are to be of eternal value to the Father, is not that of a shepherd but that of a lamb."*
> —Diane Langberg

What is narcissism?

In a Greek fable, a handsome young man named Narcissus rejects the love of others and falls in love with his own reflection in a pond, ultimately dying as a result. Dr. James Wilder comments on this story in his book *The Pandora Problem*, saying, "Real life narcissists do not like looking at themselves at all—they like looking good to others."[1]

He continues, "In modern culture, narcissism is a term for being self-centered and self-absorbed. Yet narcissism is more than being centered on 'me.' It is a dynamic game that works

---

1. E. James Wilder, *The Pandora Problem: Facing Narcissism in Leaders and Ourselves* (Carmel, IN: Deeper Walk International, 2018), 38.

according to predictable rules. As long as the narcissist sets the rules of the game...."[2]

To those who have wrestled with narcissistic leaders, being alongside those who exhibit these tendencies in their relationships and behaviors, please know this: You do not stand alone. You never have.

Leadership can be largely defined as having the ability and opportunity to influence actions and guide a group of people to accomplish a goal or objective. Leadership can be exhibited in roles defined and undefined, based on the situation and people involved. And the line can be easily crossed between having the ability and opportunity to influence actions and guide people, versus using leadership roles to control and manipulate. The tipping point is power and the use or misuse of it.

As a student of leadership behaviors and motivations, and as a seasoned leader over several decades, I have experienced narcissistic behaviors in multiple settings. The world is watching—believers and non-believers alike.

We have seen horrific public failures over the past decades: John Eagen, Bill Hybels, Ravi Zacharias, James McDonald, Ted Haggard, Jimmy Bakker, Bill Gothard, Jimmy Swaggart, Mark Driscoll, Carl Lentz, Jerry Falwell, Jr., and Tony Alamo, to name only a *few* of the most obvious ones.

In our larger cultural context, we have seen some celebrity failures as well, too many to list. As time goes on, more stories are coming to light as people share about and reflect on the fact that narcissistic leaders are everywhere.

Over the past forty years, I have encountered multiple people who caused significant damage in nonprofit organizations because of narcissistic behaviors; some simply displayed narcissistic styles, while others were specifically high-

---

2. Ibid, 38.

level and could have been diagnosed with narcissistic personality disorder.

We must be careful when dealing with mental health issues. As my friend Pete Singer from G.R.A.C.E. (Godly Response to Abuse in a Christian Environment) noted in an email on February 13, 2023: "I'm always a bit reluctant to use the term [Narcistic Personality Disorder] because it is a mental health diagnosis, and not everyone actually knows the diagnosis criteria when they talk about it. I think it sometimes results in someone who is a jerk and misuses power being called a narcissist, when they are actually a jerk who misuses power."

Indeed, there is potential to classify people as narcissistic when there are so many possible differential diagnoses to consider, such as High-Achieving Individuals, Borderline Personality Disorder, Histrionic Personality Disorder, Antisocial Personality Disorder, Obsessive-Compulsive Personality Disorder, Paranoid Personality Disorder, Schizotypal Personality Disorder, Mania or Hypomania, Substance Use Disorders, etc.

Many people function within the subclinical boundaries of behavior, but they present troublesome traits all the same. Narcissism, Psychopathy, and Machiavellianism are all part of what is referred to as "The Dark Triad," with degrees of impact in one or more of these areas in how people think, react, and manifest behaviors in life and leadership.

For this work, **narcissism may be defined as the excessive focus on self-image and a lack of empathy for others, with increasing efforts to preserve others' perception of them. All of this is centered around an imaginary reality that defines the thinking and actions of the narcissist.**

I hope readers can see the overwhelming evidence defining narcissism and how strongly this impacts faith-based and nonprofit leadership (especially in the church setting). The next step is to review options to protect the church and navigate the issue to avoid the damage done to dear souls and enable leadership to reflect the name of God in healthy ways.

Charles DeGroat wrote an excellent book called *When Narcissism Comes to Church*, where he unpacks insights and narratives that make understanding narcissism possible.

In an article from *Banner* magazine, DeGroat wrote, "I'm often asked if being a narcissist or not is like an on-off switch—either you have it or you don't. The reality is this: Narcissism exists on a spectrum. Some have the full-blown flu (NPD), others have significant symptoms (narcissistic type), and others just have the sniffles (narcissistic style)."[3]

Almost all of us can have narcissistic tendencies from time to time. Others suffer fully from personality disorder, and others simply function in a system that innocently encourages it. Just because one may occasionally show arrogance or self-serving behaviors does not necessarily dictate a casual diagnosis of Narcissism.

Drs. Kevin Weitz and William Bergquist write about hubris and narcissism, saying, "To some extent, all leaders have a bit of narcissism in them. They revel to some extent in the attention they have received from other people and are pleased that other people respect, trust, or at least follow the direction which they as leaders provide."[4]

DeGroat has defined ten features of narcissistic church leaders in his book *When Narcissism Comes to Church*:

---

3. Charles DeGroat, "Finding Narcissism in Church," *The Banner*, December 28, 2020, http://www.thebanner.org/features/2020/12/finding-narcissism-in-church.
4. Kevin Weitz and William Bergquist, "In Search of Truth I: Hubris and Narcissism," *Library of Professional Psychology*, published on July 9, 2020, https://library.psychology.edu/in-search-of-truth-i-hubris-and-narcissism/.

- All decision-making centers on them
- Impatience or lack of ability to listen to others
- Delegating without giving proper authority or with too many limits
- Feelings of entitlement
- Feeling threatened or intimidated by other talented staff
- Needing to be the best and brightest in the room
- Inconsistency and impulsiveness
- Praising and withdrawing
- Intimidating others
- Fauxnerability (fake vulnerability)[5]

These traits are consistent with other findings related to narcissism. Additionally, people with narcissism will exhibit impairments in interpersonal function, affecting their capacity to feel empathy and making it difficult or almost impossible to experience truly deep, intimate relationships.

As DeGroat highlights from the DSM-5 (*Diagnostic and Statistical Manual of Mental Disorders*, published by the American Psychiatric Association), narcissists exhibit antagonistic traits such as grandiosity, entitlement, self-centeredness, condescending attitudes, and excessive attempts to be the focus of attention.[6]

The online description for narcissism from PsychDB agrees with this definition. Specifically, to paraphrase for simplicity, narcissists exhibit the following:

---

5. Charles DeGroat, *When Narcissism Comes to Church: Healing Your Community from Emotional and Spiritual Abuse* (Downers Grove, IL: InterVarsity Press, 2020), 70.
6. American Psychiatric Association, *Diagnostic and Statistical Manual of Mental Disorders, Fifth Edition* (Washington, DC: American Psychiatric Association Publishing, 2017), 669-670.

- Grandiose sense of self-importance, e.g., exaggerates achievements and talents, and expects to be recognized as superior
- Preoccupation with fantasies of unlimited success, power, beauty, etc.
- Belief that he or she is special or unique and can only be associated with other special or unique people
- Need for excessive admiration
- Sense of entitlement, with unreasonable expectations of favorable treatment
- Interpersonally exploitative
- Lack of empathy
- Envy of others or belief that they are envious of him or her
- Arrogant or haughty behaviors[7]

Jean Twenge and W. Keith Campbell wrote in the publication of their wide-ranging study on narcissism in our culture, *Narcissism Epidemic*, "Narcissism causes almost all the things that Americans hoped high self-esteem would prevent, including aggression, materialism, lack of caring for others, and shallow values. In trying to build a society that celebrates high self-esteem, self-expression, and 'loving yourself,' Americans have inadvertently created more narcissists—and a culture that brings out the narcissistic behavior in all of us."[8]

The Mayo Clinic also highlights additional issues for the

---

7. "Narcissistic Personality Disorder," Psych DB, last modified January 27, 2024, https://www.psychdb.com/personality/narcissistic.
8. Jean M. Twenge and W. Keith Campbell, *The Narcissism Epidemic: Living in the Age of Entitlement* (New York: Simon & Schuster/Atria, 2009), 9.

narcissist. They include what has already been listed, plus the following characteristics of narcissists:

- Expect to be recognized as superior even without achievements that warrant it
- Exaggerate achievements and talents
- Monopolize conversations and belittle or look down on people they perceive as inferior
- Expect special favors and unquestioning compliance with their expectations
- Take advantage of others to get what they want
- Have an inability or unwillingness to recognize the needs and feelings of others
- Insist on having the best of everything—for instance, the best car or office[9]

Additionally, the Mayo Clinic also highlights a narcissist's response to criticism (see article for a more complete list of responses):

- Become impatient or angry when they don't receive special treatment
- Have significant interpersonal problems and easily feel slighted
- React with rage or contempt and try to belittle the other person to make themselves appear superior
- Have difficulty regulating emotions and behavior
- Experience major problems dealing with stress and adapting to change

---

9. Dana Sparks, "Narcissistic personality disorder: Inflated sense of importance," Mayo Clinic News Network, published on September 15, 2020, https://newsnetwork.mayoclinic.org/discussion/narcissistic-personality-disorder-inflated-sense-of-importance/.

- Feel depressed and moody because they fall short of perfection
- Have secret feelings of insecurity, shame, vulnerability, and humiliation[10]

While experts are mixed in their conclusions on this, it is generally understood that there is no defined cause for narcissistic behaviors and no known cure. It can be managed or treated most commonly through talk therapy, depending on the environment and relationships allowed into the mix.

Obviously, the condition of the culture since the 1970s has contributed to the increase in identified narcissistic behaviors, and there are causations in play that may include the following:

- Environment, especially family-of-origin issues
- Genetics, with inherited characteristics or traits
- Neurobiology, with brain patterns of thinking and behavior[11]

Courtney Telloian clarifies the struggles with tendencies or traits and full personality disorders. In her article, "5 Types of Narcissism," she writes, "Narcissism is closely tied to extreme self-focus, an inflated sense of self, and a strong desire for recognition and praise."[12]

Further, "Someone with overt narcissism might come across as needing to be praised and admired, exploitative,

---

10. Sparks, "Narcissistic personality disorder: Inflated sense of importance." https://newsnetwork.mayoclinic.org/discussion/narcissistic-personality-disorder-inflated-sense-of-importance/.
11. Courtney Telloian, "5 Types of Narcissism," Psych Central, updated on December 18, 2024, https://psychcentral.com/health/types-of-narcissism.
12. Ibid.

competitive, and lacking empathy...."[13] On the other hand, those with covert narcissism might demonstrate "expressions of low self-esteem, higher likelihood of experiencing anxiety, depression, and shame, introversion, insecurity or low confidence, defensiveness, avoidance, and tendency to feel or play the victim."[14]

Psychology Today writes, "Narcissism does not necessarily represent a surplus of self-esteem or of insecurity; more accurately, it encompasses a hunger for appreciation or admiration, a desire to be the center of attention, and an expectation of special treatment reflecting perceived higher status. Interestingly, research finds many highly narcissistic people often readily admit to an awareness that they are more self-centered. A high level of narcissism, not surprisingly, can be damaging in romantic, familial, or professional relationships."[15]

Narcissistic behavior is not new or unknown but appears to be significantly more common in our current culture than ever before, resulting in substantial consequences for working and family relationships. Especially troubling is what happens when there is an imbalance of power. And within caring and trusting organizations where the environment is already vulnerable, such as churches or faith-based nonprofits, narcissistic behavior can easily take hold and often leads to abuse.

---

13. Ibid.
14. Ibid.
15. "Narcissism," Basics, Psychology Today, accessed August 3, 2025, https://www.psychologytoday.com/us/basics/narcissism.

"Any type of abuse is a misuse of power, which is the ability to influence and manipulate ....Sadly, many are unaware of the power they and those around them hold, both on a micro and macro level, and ... of the power dynamics at play between different people."
—Merethe Dahl Turner

MY STORY: THE POINT OF CRISIS

Several of us felt there was trouble brewing with our congregation, the leadership, and the lead pastor.

After unsuccessfully trying to navigate potential paths toward a positive solution, and with the overwhelming stress and challenge of my executive pastor role under a narcissist, my wife and I made the difficult decision to remove ourselves from the situation.

I had to leave a few things undone, knowing the problems were still active, and the crash was coming. And this is exactly what I said to Keith when I resigned, "I am removing myself from this environment; you are in trouble, and you are going to crash."

As executive pastor, I challenged Keith one-on-one with his drinking, his erratic and whimsical behavior, his emotional attachment to young women and to any staff who were agreeable to his way of thinking, his repeated and progressive passive-aggressive attacks on anyone who didn't agree with him, his casual slide into a lackadaisical approach to leadership, and his compulsive arrogance in believing he needed to be the final word on just about all things.

His marriage appeared troubled. Groups and people within the church were isolated and divided, and families were leaving, often over something to do with him.

Keith would belittle me in front of the staff and elders and then apologize privately while still talking negatively about me when I wasn't present. Others in leadership were sharing what he was saying. It was startling and sad, watching the slow decline of a gifted man—a man I respected—as he refused any points of accountability and began to gather "compliant people" around him.

I offered him my support if he would take time off or a long sabbatical to pursue counseling or various other avenues of potential healing. He declined them all or dismissed the need; he missed several mutually agreed-upon deadlines for self-care, and he refused to see professional counselors since they were "less qualified" than him.

I caught Keith lying several times, publicly and privately. I started to pull back from any personal interaction with Keith and dealt with him only on a professional basis as much as I could. I no longer confided in him about my thoughts or feelings, as much as he badgered me to do so.

He was no longer "safe" to be around.

Several leaders, including myself, made repeated appeals for help to the elders over the previous several years. But Keith was manipulating and abusing them as well, and he met their attempts at correction with anger and attack.

The elders were taking some action behind the scenes, including communicating with the denominational district leadership.

During this time, Keith was actively working to diminish the role and responsibilities of the elders as much as possible, in addition to demeaning the chairman of the elders and questioning his credibility. He was detaching from district leadership, building the lead pastor role to be almost untouchable and without any meaningful accountability in place.

After pursuing everything I knew to do, I backed away and resigned. I finished several projects and distanced myself from the environment. We attended worship services on a sporadic basis for several months, and when we did, Keith was aloof at best and still showing signs of continued arrogant behavior. His sermons were recycled old messages, lacking passion and depth, and the staff seemed almost in fear of what could happen at any moment.

My wife and I tried to visit other congregations, but there was a sense in our prayers that God needed us to wait on any decision to stay or leave. We didn't know why, unhappy as we were, but we felt a strong sense to remain that we couldn't ignore.

POINT OF CRISIS

After one worship service, Keith asked to meet with me the next day. "It's urgent," he said.

Keith told me of his plan to resign, and he had several pages of conclusions and recommendations for the leadership during the transition. He wanted me to be available to preach on occasion and agree with his written recommendations to the board of elders. I affirmed his plan to resign and agreed to be part of a preaching rotation, but I declined to endorse his recommendations and didn't agree with his negative statements about people, specifically the chair of the elders and the denominational district superintendent.

Keith was not at all happy with my response, and he quickly concluded our meeting. I made notes afterward and notified the chair of the elders that Keith was no better than before, possibly even worse, and I anticipated he would create problems on his way out.

I learned later that Keith had misrepresented to the elders that I had agreed with his recommendations, and even further, Keith said I helped write the document with the assistance of another long-time elder.

That is also when the board of elders informed me of a formal church/district investigation into Keith's behavior. It was getting worse, and the probable recommendation would be to place him on leave or potentially terminate his employment. Keith's resignation made that action unnecessary, much to the relief of the elders and district leadership.

When we attended his final worship services and messages, Keith seemed hyper-manic and negative; he made some derogatory comments toward leadership in his sermons, especially toward the chair of the elders and me. At his "retirement" celebration, he walked through the room and left.

One month later, we received formal allegations that Keith had committed clergy sexual assault with two women in the office over an extended period of time, and one interaction was still active. After Keith's wife confronted him, he told his adult kids and several close friends.

Keith notified the two women that he was telling his family, and this news caused the women to report their experiences to the church leadership. Within days, one of the women contacted the police. After a long police investigation, criminal charges were filed. And Keith's marriage ended.

We later discovered that Keith likely had discovered the investigation; however, he was unaware of the specific issue, assuming it was the sexual relationships. This motivated him not only to resign preemptively but also to admit his actions to the family before any further news spread of the investigation.

The elders and the district superintendent asked me before the revelations to return in a part-time role as interim lead at the church. This move was due to the leadership vacuum already developing within the church and staff after just a few weeks without a lead pastor.

I wasn't confident this was the best move. I had reservations about whether taking the position would be a good thing for the church—or for me. I hesitated. But when the news about Keith was revealed, there was no doubt in our prayers that I needed to be available for this moment. And it became clear that *this* was why God still had us there.

WORST-CASE SCENARIO

We didn't realize the intensity of the battle ahead or how widespread the impact of Keith's behavior would be.

My counselor reflected that I was fighting a bear, bigger and stronger than we were led to believe. This bear had moves we didn't expect, and I was standing in the gap between this beast and the congregation.

Indeed, we were dealing with a predator—and not one in sheep's clothing. Keith was a wolf in shepherd's clothing, which is far worse. Over the coming months, I heard from others—with various analogies—that my role was to stand in the gap between evil and the church: holding things together, protecting the flock, and keeping the focus on mission.

There were only a few of us who were aware of the full reality of the situation, and even then, I doubt we knew it all. Those people included me, the chair of the elders, the secretary of the elders, the church attorney, and the denominational district superintendent. To their credit, in the face of such a strong force, we all stood together in the gap. We took substantial hits, and some of them were deeply personal and hurtful.

Yes, we could have done a few things differently, and we made mistakes, but we also did a lot of things correctly. It was all happening so quickly. Beyond those few people, others heard bits and pieces of things. Those incomplete narratives gave rise to grand assumptions from various sides, filling in the gaps with gossip and guesses. The battle lines being drawn were complex and intense.

The details of incidents with the women were shocking, and Keith's continued actions were even more so, with specific ongoing details outlined in temporary restraining orders filed by the women. And Keith's family shared additional details that were troubling, especially the events and activities leading up to and immediately after his confession. The trauma and pain he caused for so many were beyond comprehension.

When charges were filed, the accusations and details in the police report were difficult to read. None of us had any idea it was so brutal or complex.

At one point, I counted over twenty considerations in this situation to maneuver: the board of elders (divided in their thinking and struggling to agree); the church staff (divided in their thinking, with several resigning); the congregation (divided in their thinking, with people leaving and coming back); Keith and his close friends; the women and their families; several other staff women who were "groomed" but not approached yet; several other women who were approached but resisted; Keith's family; consultants working with the church; denominational leadership; legal counsel; the insurance company; the police detective and county attorney; former staff and church members speaking out; the interim transition team; the pastoral search team; media reporters; and on top of all that, my own feelings, family, and friends.

People were voicing all sorts of things via email, texts, phone calls, meetings, social media, and letters.

Our district superintendent said we needed to shepherd others in their journey at the same time as we were shepherding our own.

No one seemed to have all the information needed to draw any good conclusions or tell a complete narrative, much less define a clear path forward. And almost everyone wanted to see someone—anyone—held responsible for what happened, especially when the offender was no longer part of the community. It seemed people wanted others to know about and share the deep pain we were all feeling.

As leaders, we couldn't share the facts with just anyone who asked, especially topics related to human resource considerations. We also couldn't share things publicly when there was an active police investigation, with Keith and one of the women threatening litigation.

Some people were so demeaning and demanding, believing their limited perspective of the situation was somehow the standard for how we should handle the situation.

Keith asked to speak to the entire congregation and then to the board of elders so he could apologize and explain. Both requests were denied. We said we would accept a statement or letter from him, but not a personal appearance.

Advocates of Keith were confronting me before, between, and after worship services, and by phone calls and messages. The church's refusal to let Keith speak led to a threat of litigation against the church, which was his second threat in several months.

One of the women also wanted to address the congregation to tell her story of what happened. We offered to make her narrative available to people in print and via video, but we did not want to impose this narrative on anyone and everyone. Some people didn't want to know the details, and it was too early to share those details while formal investigations were in process.

Stepping back and looking at this entire situation, there is no question in my mind: We were, indeed, doing battle with a bear.

CHAPTER TWO
NARCISSISM IN CHRISTIAN LEADERSHIP

In their book *Overcoming the Dark Side of Leadership*, Gary McIntosh and Samuel Rima included a list of the top five issues that bring out the dark side in leaders: compulsivity, paranoia, codependency, passive-aggressive behavior, and narcissism, in which they define narcissism as "various combinations of intense ambitiousness, grandiose fantasies, feelings of inferiority, and overdependence on external admiration and acclaim."[1]

DeGroat also wrote, "In the end, this is a conversation for pastors and laity, for seminary professors and church planting assessors, for elder boards and mission organizations, for mercy ministries and activist organizations, for therapists and spiritual directors. Together, we can imagine what it might mean to follow in the way of the One who refused to grasp,

---

1. Alexander Lowan as cited by Gary L. McIntosh and Samuel D. Rima, *Overcoming the Dark Side of Leadership: How to Become an Effective Leader by Confronting Potential Failures* (Grand Rapids: Baker Books, 2007), 98.

who became a servant, whose Kingship does not demand loyalty but invites humble followers to walk in the way."[2]

In their study, Craig and Carolyn Williford list several signs of narcissism in clergy, which can be translated to any executive leadership of a nonprofit or faith-based organization. They define character traits of narcissists, including "impatience or a lack of ability to listen to others," "feelings of entitlement," "delegating without giving proper authority or with too many limits," and "needing to be the best and brightest in the room."[3]

Dr. Heintz Kohut capitalizes on more narcissistic tendencies, particularly as they apply to relationships. A narcissist may showcase "an inability to form and maintain significant relationships, a lack of humor, empathy, or sense of proportion, unaccountable rage, and pathological lying."[4]

Drs. Darrel Puls and R. Glenn Ball conducted a study and presented a paper in 2015 to the American Association of Christian Counselors, subsequently publishing a book on narcissism in clergy.

When it was later revealed that the study methodology was incorrectly applied and its results were flawed, Puls worked with the publisher to pull any remaining copies and rework a revision that was less dependent upon the study and more focused on his experience as a Christian counselor and pastor.

His book *Let Us Prey* is a significant work, even without

---

[2]. Charles DeGroat, "Narcissistic Leadership in the Church," A Foundation for Theological Education, John Wesley Foundation, published on October 13, 2021, https://johnwesleyfellows.org/perspectives/narcissistic-leadership-in-the-church/.

[3]. Craig Williford and Carolyn Williford, *How to Treat a Staff Infection: Resolving Problems in Your Church or Ministry* (Grand Rapids: Baker Books, 2006), 104-110.

[4]. Heintz Kohut, *The Analysis of the Self: A Systematic Approach to the Psychoanalytic Treatment of Narcissistic Personality Disorders* (New York: International University Press, 1976), 23, 263.

the study results. While the research done with Dr. Ball through the Presbyterian Church of Canada using the Netherlands Narcissism Scale was fundamentally skewed, their personal experiences, research from other studies and authors, and conclusions are worth noting. (I should add that Dr. Puls was immediately responsive when the problem was discovered, and he acted to make corrections with a high level of integrity. While the study findings were less than scientific in application, their research and conclusions warrant some reflection.)

In a preliminary report to the American Association of Christian Counselors, Puls comments about the narcissistic pastor, "The constant need for recognition as an authoritative expert, the lack of empathy, the need to be right, the inability to forgive, the drive for revenge, and the willingness to manipulate, use, and throw away parishioners is the antithesis of Christ. It poisons the gospel message and destroys faith in God and each other . . . Equally damaging is the narcissist's need for a scapegoat on whom to vent his or her rage. Since the narcissist pastor cannot conceive of being wrong or making a mistake, he or she must always have someone else to blame for what goes wrong . . . Often that scapegoat is a subordinate who the narcissist will isolate and attack relentlessly until the subordinate leaves, at which time another scapegoat is needed. If there is no subordinate, the narcissist pastor is likely to find multiple parishioners to attack one or two at a time. The attacks leave the targeted individuals bewildered, discouraged, and sometimes with their faith destroyed."[5]

This is an accurate definition of how narcissists work and the negative outcomes of their leadership. In a nonprofit

---

5. R. Glenn Ball and Darrell Puls, "Frequency of Narcissistic Personality Disorder in Pastors: A Preliminary Study" (report, American Association of Christian Counselors, Nashville, September 26, 2015).

setting, often with volunteers, the impact of this kind of behavior can be deeply impactful and will leave scars on staff and those who are volunteering their time for the sake of the organization and mission.

Dr. James Wilder also highlights how narcissism in faith-based settings is a critical issue facing our culture. He has written several books regarding spiritual development and brain science, including *Pandora Problem, The Other Half of Church*, and *Rare Leadership*.

In his writings, Wilder notes the core challenge: the soil of our churches. In *The Other Half of Church*, he explains, "The church has both a culture and an infection . . . The culture of the church is its relational soil, and the infection thrives in depleted soil. A chain of events has left us with exhausted soil that bears little fruit."[6]

Further, he writes: "Relationally impoverished soil leaves a community vulnerable to the spread of narcissism, especially in positions of leadership and influence. Enriching the soil is the only long-term solution. We can remove the narcissists from their positions of influence, but without adding the essential soil nutrients, the infection will return. The consequence of this disease devastates churches and families."[7]

This is why it's so important to continually nurture the "soil" of our church communities, not only dealing with narcissism but also ensuring that church members feel seen, heard, and like they are part of a strong community.

While there are many examples of good leadership and healthy organizations, there are just as many examples of unhealthy situations where narcissistic behaviors are prevalent.

---

6. E. James Wilder and Michael Hendricks, *The Other Half of the Church: Christian Community, Brain Science, and Overcoming Spiritual Stagnation* (Chicago: Moody Publishers, 2020), 156.
7. Ibid 156.

In two larger urban congregations in the Upper Midwest that both suffered under a narcissistic key leader—with assessments done through the parachurch organization Vital Church Ministry—we can start to identify some similarities within the system of those congregations. With permission from the church leadership and Vital Church, I reviewed their confidential internal reports and noted similarities. Specifically:

- There were leadership issues and failures over long periods of time, where staff and church members left after having failed to call out the bad behaviors or after having called out the bad behaviors without consequence.
- There was a lack of meaningful accountability and structure in place, and the churches tolerated problems for the sake of peace and continued perceived progress in the mission. In a church setting, it can be seen as "go along to get along." Over time, this approach became harmful.
- There seemed to be low effort expended toward fellowship and evangelism, even though it was a stated and felt need. The focus and emphasis of time, energy, and funds were toward events or settings where the narcissist felt affirmed. In the case of key pastoral leaders as narcissists, this resulted in significant attention on weekend services or educational settings that highlighted the significance of the pastor as leader or "sage," all done at the expense of activities outside of the preaching or teaching experience, such as small groups, fellowship events, or missional activities.
- There appeared to be a general acquiescence or acceptance of less-than-ideal behaviors for the sake

of perceived benefits of good teaching and preaching. Not just the feeling of "what good would it do" to complain, bad behavior was accepted and/or ignored, with complaints labeled as nonsense and complainers as troublesome.

- In both situations, there seemed to be minimal or absent skills in healthy conflict resolution or transformation, and conflict was minimized by dominant micro-management. Thus, conflict became a contest of right/wrong or strong/weak. In our culture today, we often notice some of the same patterns.
- In both situations, there was a loss of mission and/or a loss of a gospel-driven perspective. This is something we continue to see in our culture as well: Christian life in an affluent Western society is a challenge, and church members are faced with options that can minimize involvement and increase drift.
- In both situations, while friendly and positive, the congregations seemed weak in welcoming and assimilating new people into the community.
- In most situations where narcissistic behaviors begin in minor ways and escalate over time (certainly in these two examples), the churches established systems to covertly discourage people from raising issues or concerns, and in these settings, people didn't feel safe to speak up about it.

CHAPTER THREE
SUBSEQUENT TRUTHS

"The acts of the flesh are obvious: sexual immorality, impurity and debauchery; idolatry and witchcraft; hatred, discord, jealousy, fits of rage, selfish ambition, dissensions, factions and envy; drunkenness, orgies, and the like. I warn you, as I did before, that those who live like this will not inherit the kingdom of God. But the fruit of the Spirit is love, joy, peace, forbearance, kindness, goodness, faithfulness, gentleness, and self-control."
—Galatians 5:19–23, NIV

Based on what I learned thus far about narcissistic behaviors and examples of narcissism in leadership, some truths are evident:

- We all have narcissistic tendencies, usually governed in humility and community; it is possible to exhibit narcissistic behaviors without having Narcissistic Personality Disorder. However,

narcissism is on the rise due to the growing sense of entitlement and individualism in our culture.
- The narcissistic person is not evil but can act in evil ways; the person manifesting narcissistic behavior is not evil either but *will* (not just can but will) act in evil ways. Think addict and their substance of choice.
- Narcissism is *not* the same as being self-centered or selfish; there is a fine distinction here. Most narcissists do not need to be the center of attention or demand focus on themselves; on the contrary, their desire is to be recognized and appreciated as the best in the room: the smartest, the brightest, the most educated, the most experienced, the most capable. The narcissist does not need for people to focus on him or her, although it is OK and understandable if they do; the narcissist desires for those who do look at them to see the narcissist favorably. Thus, narcissists will shape the narrative and bend the facts to make it seem they are the best and the brightest when studies have shown they are usually as average as everyone else (see Twenge and Campbell's *The Narcissism Epidemic*).
- Narcissism is a progressive pattern of behavior, usually over a long period of time, unless there are systems in place to monitor and contain any negative behaviors. Left unchecked and with minimal consequences if caught, the narcissist will cause great damage and ultimately "crash."
- Narcissists are not necessarily liars, at least not intentionally or knowingly. Most people who exhibit a high level of narcissism will create a fictional reality that allows them to appear

smarter than everyone else and explains why they think the way they do about people and situations. While half-truths or exaggerations to everyone else, narcissists believe their statements are truth-based on this perceived reality. Thus, it is challenging to argue or debate with a narcissist because people are not just confronting a moment but also calling into question the narcissist's entire understanding of how things are, at least to them.

While narcissists are not necessarily liars, those around them are not necessarily overly gullible either. They find themselves believing only what they have context to understand; thus, people can deny the obvious truth that seems outside of their ability to comprehend or apprehend it. For example, it's difficult to believe a respected senior pastor is preaching from scripture and making so much sense, only to hear he or she is abusing multiple people. In one situation, the pastor was brilliant and articulate, and he would preach on Sunday and return home to abuse his family, often in a drunken stupor. This is why a narcissist is often referred to as a "crazy-maker." The narcissist makes everyone else question what they feel or what they perceive.

Wilder writes in *The Pandora Problem*, "By changing history and recoloring the details, narcissists create their own reality . . . Eventually, creating one's own reality leads to believing one's own lies. The next step is coming down hard on others who do not agree. Changing reality is especially useful for narcissists after they have hurt others. Instead of sharing pain with those they have hurt, narcissists change the story and then blame their victims."[1]

- Narcissists in any organization can bring about great progress with any cause. They often can be larger-than-life in the way they present themselves, which can be helpful in some situations. However, they can cause great damage as a result, misusing and abusing those around them—often those people closest to them, which results in damaging many relationships.

There is an ongoing discussion in business literature about how effective leaders need to exhibit some narcissistic tendencies for them to be successful in their roles. There is some basis of truth in this debate, and some good examples to draw from, but it is rare for leadership (the leader, staff, and governing board) to be able to balance this behavior and keep this leader from destroying talented people or an amazing organization.

One may raise the question of whether there is a significant difference between courageous confidence and outright pride or hubris. It can happen when the balance is kept and the organization remains healthy, but it is rarer than imagined.

- Systems of accountability and evaluation must be more than casual, and those systems must be frequently checked and adjusted. Good accountability and evaluation are dynamic in nature, with good boundaries and multiple levels of meaningful accountability in place. For most,

---

1. E. James Wilder, *The Pandora Problem: Facing Narcissism in Leaders and Ourselves* (Carmel, IN: Deeper Walk International, 2018), 92.

those parameters and boundaries need to be in place from the start of the relationship, managed with grace, courage, and humble authority.
- Narcissistic behaviors will squash community, which limits both fellowship and evangelism. For narcissism to take root, isolation and filtered communication are necessary. (Note that the narcissist tends to only be in a community they can control or lead.) The narcissist will often isolate groups of people, such as leadership teams, and attempt to control communication by filtering information through their perspective of reality applied.
- Narcissism is limited when there is a strong sense of community, a commitment to each other, relationships that are governed by humility and transparency, and a sense of mission that is greater than the sum of those involved. Community and humility are key to keeping narcissism in check.
- Narcissism requires a focus of attention, either positive or negative, which is called "narcissist supply." Remove or limit the attention, and the narcissist will either be contained or move on to places where the need for attention will be met.
- Narcissists create codependent people, drawing them into the circle of manipulation. Most people will not realize there is a problem until it is too late to resist or flee (see Paul Meier and Robert Wise's book *Crazy Makers*).
- To avoid addressing narcissistic behaviors may seem like a gracious and compassionate choice, but it will ultimately harm the person, the organization, and the talented and passionate people associated with the organization. It may be

a challenge to confront bad behavior, and it may be followed by a painful season, but there is a greater cost to avoiding the problems for the sake of peace or the perceived success of the organization.
- There is no cure for narcissism, only coping mechanisms for them and those around them. Truth-telling in a direct but caring way can be helpful if there is any sense of "others" in the narcissist's frame of reference. Narcissists can be effective and successful in whatever they decide to accomplish, but that success always comes at a cost. In a caring and trusting environment, the cost can be human and emotional, not just tangible.

Often, if left unchecked and without careful management, unbridled narcissism can result in extremely damaging emotional and even physical abuse, which can easily transition into sexual abuse or assault.

In my experience, and in studies of leadership behavior, we need to look for tendencies toward any of the negative and positive signs, both the tangible and intangible ones, as much as possible.

CHAPTER FOUR
ABUSE, HUBRIS, AND POWER

"But studies also show that once people assume positions of power, they're likely to act more selfishly, impulsively, and aggressively, and they have a harder time seeing the world from other people's points of view.... The skills most important to obtaining power and leading effectively are the very skills that deteriorate once we have power."
—Dacher Keltner

Word Definitions

Abuse
Noun: 1) a corrupt practice or custom; 2) improper or excessive use or treatment; 3) language that condemns or vilifies usually unjustly, intemperately, and angrily; 4) physical maltreatment; Verb: 1) to put to a wrong or improper use; 2) to use excessively; 3) to use or treat so as to injure or damage; 4) to attack in words.[1]

---

1. *Merriam-Webster*, s.v. "abuse *(n.)* *(v.)*," accessed August 3, 2025, https://www.merriam-webster.com/dictionary/abuse.

Hubris
Noun: 1) exaggerated pride or self-confidence. "... a dangerous character flaw...."[2]

Power
Noun: 1a) ability to act or produce an effect, ability to get extra-base hits; capacity for being acted upon or undergoing an effect; 1b) legal or official authority, capacity, or right; 2a) possession of control, authority, or influence over others; 2b) one having such power; 2c) a controlling group; 3a) physical might; 3b) mental or moral efficacy; 3c) political control or influence.[3]

Abuse. While not exclusive, I believe narcissistic behavior is the on-ramp where abuse is nurtured, whether spiritual, emotional, financial, physical, or sexual. The tendencies and systems that fuel the narcissist are the very factors that lead to abusive opportunities, usually discovered in hindsight after something terrible has happened. I can attest to this point, as a survivor of not one but two supervisors in ministry who were narcissistic and abusive in extreme ways.

Pete Singer and Mike Sloan from G.R.A.C.E. (Godly Response to Abuse in a Christian Environment) have educated many on the patterns of abuse that can occur in nonprofit and religious settings. According to their research, it happens more times than we would care to comprehend.

Over the past several years, G.R.A.C.E. has responded to hundreds of inquiries worldwide from churches and faith-

---

2. *Merriam-Webster*, s.v. "hubris *(n.)*," accessed August 3, 2025, https://www.merriam-webster.com/dictionary/hubris.
3. *Merriam-Webster*, s.v. "power *(n.)*," accessed August 3, 2025, https://www.merriam-webster.com/dictionary/power.

based organizations that are facing the abuse of children and/or adults, and the public is becoming increasingly aware that the trusting culture of the faith community is often the perfect setting for grooming and abuse to take place.

Their definition speaks volumes: "Abuse occurs when a person in a position of power and trust uses that position to exploit or violate a person who is more vulnerable. Abuse can be physical, sexual, emotional, spiritual, financial, etc. . . . Clergy sexual abuse occurs when a pastor or spiritual leader crosses sexual boundaries with a person under their spiritual care or supervision."[4]

Leadership at G.R.A.C.E. write about emotional and spiritual abuse, "Healthy communities respect appropriate relational and emotional boundaries. As much as leaders are called to impart and embody wisdom and take responsibility for decisions, godly leaders do not domineer, control, or usurp agency from others. Healthy leaders focus on setting an example, equipping, listening, valuing others, and empowering others instead of making all the decisions alone or ordering the lives of others . . . All people are made in the image of God with inherent dignity and worth. There is never any justification to objectify, insult, demean, humiliate, threaten, shame, or rage at another person, no matter what they have done. When we use our power to dehumanize or insult or objectify others (especially those who are more vulnerable or downtrodden), we are ultimately insulting God."[5]

We must raise awareness and wave caution flags to everyone in settings where the vulnerable are involved. But

---

4. PowerPoint presentation, Saint Paul, MN, September 2023.
5. G.R.A.C.E., *Emotional and Spiritual Abuse* (handout given at leadership training presentation in Saint Paul, MN, September 2023).

even more so, we must do all we can to prevent predators from being in a position of power where abuse can be considered.

An educated community is a safe community. It's time faith-based organizations learn more about abuse and narcissistic systems to help keep our communities safe.

G.R.A.C.E. defines some common abuse dynamics that come into play, and you can see similarities in the definitions of abuse settings and narcissistic tendencies:

- Power and Vulnerability
- Trust and Community
- Entitlement and Dehumanization or Objectification
- Deception and Manipulation
- Isolation and Powerlessness
- Fear, Secrecy, and Silence[6]

Hubris. It is a fair consideration to compare narcissism with hubris, and some leadership experts are now exploring this differentiation, especially as it relates to power and abuse.

Dr. Sarosh Asad and Dr. Eugene Sadler-Smith have written an excellent paper on this topic, comparing the two and exploring the dynamics that come into play with leadership settings. They write, "Hubris is a grandiose sense of self, characterized by disrespectful attitudes toward others and a misperception of one's place in the world . . . It is an acquired condition triggered by accession to a position of significant power, amplified by overestimations of one's

---

6. Singer and Sloan, "Leadership Training: Creating a Culture of Protection" (PowerPoint presentation).

abilities based on prior success and facilitated by lack of constraints regarding how a leader exercises power."[7]

Asad and Sadler-Smith reference Bertram Russell's *History of Western Philosophy* by citing, when the check on pride is removed from any leader, "a further step is taken on the road toward a certain kind of madness—the intoxication with power," which Russell believes to be "the greatest danger of our time."[8] Asad and Sadler-Smith continue, "Power achievement and accumulation is the ultimate goal for hubristic leaders, but narcissists use power to construct a reality with their self-centered and flamboyant persona."[9]

Asad and Sadler-Smith conclude, "Detrimental influences of such leaders can be averted by the presence of a strong executive team and outside directors and by promoting distributed and shared models of leadership . . . "

As we will highlight later, the need for accountability and checks/balances is necessary when dealing with any leadership dysfunction, especially one such as hubris and narcissism: "Being skillful with rhetoric, narcissistic leaders take advantage of the power that comes with symbolic status, abusing followers' belief systems and psychological well-being during the process."[10]

Power. You may have heard these quotes (or sentiments similar to them): "Power tends to corrupt; absolute power

---

7. Sarosh Asad and Eugene Sadler-Smith, "Differentiating Leader Hubris and
   Narcissism on the Basis of Power," *Sage Journals* 16, no. 1 (February 2020): 4 https://doi.org/10.1177/1742715019885763.
8. Ibid, 4.
9. Ibid, 24.
10. Ibid, 21.

corrupts absolutely" (Lord Acton), and "It is much safer to be feared than loved" (Machiavelli).

There is great danger when some elements of personality are coupled with the mantle of power, whether real or perceived. Many studies have been written about the use (and abuse) of power in leadership. It is worthy of our interest, but suffice to say, power is an area of profound challenge and can be used well—but too often, it is not.

One narcissistic leader was discovered to be acting in distinct contrast to a public and often discussed "rule" of conduct by leaders of that organization. When confronted by a board member, the leader responded, "I changed the rules," and walked away uncontested.

In psychological science, power is defined "as one's capacity to alter another person's condition or state of mind by providing or withholding resources—such as food, money, knowledge, and affection—or administering punishments, such as physical harm, job termination, or social ostracism."[11]

Dr. Dacher Keltner wrote in *The Power Paradox*, "We tend to believe that attaining power requires force, deception, manipulation, and coercion. Indeed, we might even assume that positions of power demand this kind of conduct—that to run smoothly, society needs leaders who are willing and able to use power this way. As seductive as these notions are, they are dead wrong . . . Years of research suggest that empathy and social intelligence are vastly more important to acquiring and exercising power than are force, deception, or terror . . . But studies also show that once people assume positions of power, they're likely to act more selfishly, impulsively, and aggressively, and they have a harder time seeing the world from

---

11. Dacher Keltner, "The Power Paradox," *Greater Good Magazine*, published on December 1, 2007, https://greatergood.berkeley.edu/article/item/power_paradox.

other people's points of view . . . The skills most important to obtaining power and leading effectively are the very skills that deteriorate once we have power."[12]

Maybe power is not the issue as much as it is our flawed, sinful nature.

Dr. Diane Langberg wrote in *Redeeming Power: Understanding Authority and Abuse in the Church*, "Research on power and compassion/empathy has shown that elevated social power is associated with a diminished reciprocal emotional response to another's sufferings. In other words, the more power a person holds in relation to other people, the less empathy they will have."[13]

This seems to contradict what we would consider logical in a nonprofit and/or faith-based organization, where people are not just the means for accomplishing the mission but also the very mission itself. The sense of power can often dominate and diminish our sense of compassion. The lack of love is often seen, while not overtly in words, but covertly in actions.

This summary of power as a leader is significant, especially in the setting of a faith-based community. Langberg adds, "As we get involved in caring for others, caught up in the drama of their lives, keenly aware of their pressing needs, we can easily be seduced into forgetting that we are first a sheep before we are a shepherd. If we forget that we are a sheep, we will become focused on getting others to move, change, and grow while failing to seek out our Shepherd and the green pastures and still waters He has for us."[14]

Further, she writes, "A shepherd who is not first a lamb is a dangerous shepherd and has ceased to follow the Good

---

12. Ibid.
13. Diane Langberg, *Redeeming Power: Understanding Authority and Abuse in the Church* (Grand Rapids, MI: Brazos Press/Baker Publishing, 2020): 132.
14. Ibid, 150.

Shepherd. Our primary identity in life, if we are to be of eternal value to the Father, is not that of a shepherd but that of a lamb. Take heed lest you be seduced . . . Do not presume to do the work of God from any other foundation other than an ongoing relationship with him."[15]

Clergy and faith-based leaders, and those around them, please take note.

It is disappointing to find that so many leaders have no idea the level of power held within a position or in someone's personality. And it is even more discouraging to see people beaten down and laid bare by the misuse of power when character and humility are not part of the mix.

"Integrity: choosing courage over comfort; choosing what is right over what is fun, fast, or easy; and choosing to practice our values rather than simply professing them."
—Brené Brown

---

15. Ibid, 150.

MY STORY: PROCESSING WHAT HAPPENED

I had my questions about the accusations and situation, to be sure. I wondered why the victims didn't speak out sooner or say no when the abuse was happening. And why didn't we see some of this as it was taking place?

I believe those questions are a normal part of processing what happened. Yet, I also have come to understand the depth of Keith's manipulation and deception toward the women, but also toward the rest of us too. My lack of understanding and desire to know more information has little value or bearing when compared to the pain of those involved, and I refused to harbor these questions any longer than I needed to dismiss them.

Keith is fully to blame, and he manipulated and coerced the victims and the system in brutal and deeply disturbing ways. There is little doubt in my mind about what happened, and I believe the victims without pause. There is no blame or shame in my heart for those who suffered under Keith's sinful behavior.

As a leader but also as a Christian, I will grieve over this as long as I live, feeling the horror of what was done to specific people and this congregation, wishing I had known and could have done something to stop it. I have thought many times, *if only* . . .

Even if it seems legitimate to ask questions of those making the accusations (it is *not*, by the way), they also should be asked of the leadership, both staff and elders, or the congregation and family/friends who were closest to Keith. Questions like, "Why didn't *you* say something sooner?" Or, "If you did but saw nothing happening from the leadership, why not say it more strongly and to more people?" Overall, the question is, why didn't more of us say no to the overly dominant and demeaning behavior of Keith when we encountered it?

One leader witnessed Keith behaving in ways that were contrary to his vocalized standards. When this leader asked about it, Keith responded, "I changed the rules," and walked away. How was that OK?

Another leader repeatedly listened to Keith tell obvious lies about this situation, with new levels of deception being spread with every conversation. Yet, this leader continued to meet with Keith in hopes of a restored relationship and some changed behavior. How was that OK?

Another former leader, in tears, shared, "Everything he says is a lie," but he continued to blame others for what happened because of what Keith told him. How was that OK?

Several friends and church members witnessed Keith's manic behavior at a holiday service and commented afterward, "It seemed like he was drunk." But nothing further was said. How was that OK?

Some people closest to Keith caught him drinking during a worship service and confronted him about the behavior, but they told no one else about what they saw or Keith's response. How was that OK?

I personally should have contacted not just the elders with

my concerns but also the district superintendent to report what I saw and the impact it was having on the congregation. But I didn't. And I should have spoken up louder when I resigned, but I didn't. How was that OK?

Throughout the stories of the accusations and the stories from those whom Keith approached over the past ten years, the consistent thread was the tactics he used. His approach was always the same, which lends credibility to the narrative given by the victims and potential victims.

Even as things were becoming known, Keith was found behaving in similar ways with another woman. There is little possibility for this to have been coordinated as a plan "to bring him down," as some people had said.

As we know from past situations, no personal narrative is without some details being forgotten or confused, especially when significant trauma is taking place. Few of us take notes or document details when in trouble; in most cases, we are just trying to survive and do the best we can.

We dare not forget this fact: Keith admitted to his sinful actions. He confessed his extramarital sexual affairs to his family and friends, in his statement to the police, and in court.

Regardless of any real or perceived "cause" or distorted definition of the action taking place, he was supposed to be the adult in the room, the one who stands strong in the face of temptation and resists in the name of Christ—as a leader, husband, father, grandfather, Christian, and ordained minister of the gospel. But he didn't.

As Keith was issuing words of apology, repentance, and seeking forgiveness, he continued in his sin. There appeared to be little or no remorse. That should be enough for us to develop a strong understanding of the truth, and there is no need to entertain any excuses or attempts to share blame on his part.

CHAPTER FIVE
TOOLS FOR PREVENTION

To get to a healthy blend of real-life behaviors and balance, I encourage leadership on every level of an organization to put the following in place. I've listed these recommendations below in what I believe should be an order of importance. See Appendix A for more details.

Accountability and Boundaries: Define real points of accountability, with consequences for success and failure. Accountability need not be punitive in nature but instead *developmental* and *affirming*. Some boundaries can be set *for* the person, and some set *by* the person. Overall, it is the reality that no one is acting or allowed to act on their own. We should be encouraging transparency.

Mentoring Relationships: The more responsibilities and visibility of the role, the more vital it is to have mentoring relationships. Ideally, you should have the following mentors: at least one person "above" you (someone in a higher role or who is more mature/experienced) to meet with semiannually, at least one person "behind" you (to share ideas and ask questions) to meet with monthly, and at least one person "alongside" you (a peer and good friend) to meet with weekly. Key to all of this is asking open rather than closed questions. These relationships can be considered "mentoring discipleship."

Mentoring is an overused term, and in this culture, more people are wish to be mentored than agree to be a mentor. Our experiences and culture have made serving as a mentor seem almost overwhelming and something that requires a whole set of attitudes and knowledge. But in the culture of faith and community, mentoring doesn't need to be as scary as it may first appear.

Mentoring and being mentored is simply being alongside one another as a friend and as an encourager, not only to bring out the best in others but also to remind one another of who we really are. In that process, both mentor and mentee benefit.

Continuing Education: Many career tracks require some form of continuing education, especially when these are positions of responsibility, trust, and power. It has long puzzled me why pastoral or faith-based leadership is not required to participate in continuing education, no matter the status of titles or education.

A church or organization could require a specific number of hours each year. If it's not based on a denominational standard, the board of the specific organization or church could encourage and/or require it.

With so many online resources available now, like no other time in history, the organizations could easily manage the requirement, and there would be countless benefits to the local organizations and the long-term health of the faith communities.

This requirement could be integrated into churches and organizations easily, especially since many colleges offer both online and on-site courses for adults. But know that face-to-face classes are always preferred, as online interaction allows for some deception that cannot happen in person.

Truly, if a leader resists continuing education, is this not a marker of concern about teachability?

Check-Ins with Key Relationships: For any leader, regular check-ins are needed with spouse and children, best friends, and key staff. Again, they're not punitive or invasive in nature but developmental and preventive. If boards and supervisors take the time to do a quick check-in with the people who are around the leaders regularly, we may be able to catch issues and celebrate successes much more often.

In the business setting, this can be referred to as a "360 Review," drawing in feedback from multiple sources around the leader. The scope of evaluation and feedback needs to be wider, including not just those who work around this person but also those who live with them.

Define Life Clues: This recommendation is more subjective than objective, but still important. If possible, define some life clues that may point to an issue or challenge in the leader's life.

The clues may be the tone and words being used with family and staff, or even to the organization, that can point to stress or personal challenges. A clue may be the use of time, whether too much in the office or too little, too much "invisible" time, and not enough time around people, or even taking too much or too little time on tasks. All these things serve as clues that something may be amiss in the life of the leader.

There may be some life clues about moods or attitudes, how personal relationships are being managed, or even financial clues (stress over vehicle or home repairs, avoiding spending money or spending too much money all at once, etc.).

Ask Key Questions: If leaders are trying to hide something from others, or if they are playing games with behavior, then they will take a defensive position when people ask them questions regularly. However, I've found that most healthy leaders enjoy being asked and welcome the opportunity to talk less about issues of work and more about concerns of life. This is a relational piece to leadership development and should happen at least monthly.

Annual Evaluations: Evaluations need to be real and measurable, and they should include both role execution and spiritual development. The board and denominational leadership should be included as much as possible in evaluations. In some cases, leaders may wish to include a counselor to assess mental and spiritual health or well-being.

Sadly, many organizations do not provide annual evaluations for their staff and leadership. Or they do not provide role descriptions, which are foundational for good evaluations but also needed for objective determinations of progress or areas for development.

Code of Conduct: Due to the visibility of the role, faith-based leadership needs an explicit code of conduct, with real criteria of behavior and a real set of consequences to back up the expectations. Without this, there can be no meaningful accountability when parameters are not clear.

Others have created a set of personal rules that guide their behaviors to protect life and ministry. While never formal, my spouse and I have developed some practices that have served this need. Here are a few of ours as an example:

- Discuss meeting schedules with your spouse and include all meetings, locations, and general topics expected.
- Never meet with a person alone unless there are others nearby. Public meetings are ideal, but if a private office meeting is needed, it has been my practice to make sure someone else remains in the office area for the duration of the meeting. If someone makes a surprise visit, never sit down or get comfortable. Also, indicate the need to keep the contact short.
- If alone in a car going to or from an event or activity, get permission from a spouse or parent and be transparent about the destination and who was present.
- If there is a one-on-one scheduled off-site meeting, always let your spouse or coworker know who will be at the meeting, the purpose of the meeting, the location of the meeting, and when the meeting will be over. (My own practice was to let my administrative assistant know the same information. When I arrive at the meeting, I call or text my spouse that I have arrived, and when I have finished, I call or text that I'm done. If there was anything unusual to note, I made sure to tell my spouse and coworker immediately.)

- If someone pays for registration to an event or covers the cost of a study book with cash, I never accept it unless I have someone else there to witness it and note why it was paid to me. Never handle cash alone and always note the details immediately.
- If there is any history of complications or problems with certain people, do not agree to meetings with them one-on-one. Ask a coworker or spouse to participate, and if this condition is not acceptable, don't agree to the meeting.
- If a Human Resources-related meeting is needed, never hold it alone and always have a representative from HR or someone trusted by both people present. Advise them in advance of the topic to be addressed and ask for their feedback after the meeting, if possible.
- After meetings of any consequence, make a note of the length, topic, and any action items. This note does not need to be intensely detailed, but enough to be able to recall the outcomes of the meeting if asked later.
- Take a spiritual retreat for private thinking and reading at least once per year. If possible, take the retreats alone. But a retreat with your spouse is also good—to enjoy the quiet time of reading and studying together.
- If anything happens in the daily workflow that feels weird, whether with a coworker or client, tell someone and document the incident. Expect the best but assume the worst, and always be prepared to answer for anything said or done.
- Always have at least one highly trusted person in your life, someone who is unimpressed by your

title and able to speak into your attitudes, behaviors, and personal life. Meet with that person weekly or biweekly to talk about life and work. Find someone who can tell if you are "faking it," and make sure they have permission to tell others about it if needed.
- Many developing sins can be traced to a series of moments when secrecy is permitted, isolation is allowed, and compromises are made. Do whatever is possible to prevent any secrecy and isolation from taking place. Note that many amazing careers of effective ministry can be traced to a long pattern of transparency, careful personal decisions, and healthy accountability.

Others may develop similar or more detailed accountability rules, but these have been vital to my practice and life.

The National Association of Evangelicals has an excellent code of conduct, as does the organization Christianityworks. See Appendix B for more details.

There are multiple examples of good conduct and strong consequences in many organizations, but each will vary based on work standards and settings. But make no mistake: Conduct is important, and expectations need to be clear.

In the faith-based or Christian organization where leadership—good or bad—has eternal consequences and global impact, some minimal points should be included:

- Expectation of Bible-based behaviors in the whole of life, as a leader, as a Christian, and as an example to others
- Professional behavior as a leader and as a Christian (unique to the ministry setting)

- Personal behavior as a leader and as a Christian
- Moral behavior as a leader and as a Christian
- Financial integrity, both at work and at home
- Ministry property and resources
- Accountability on various levels
- Reporting and expected responses
- Authority and consequences

In the absence of any expectations of conduct or standards of behavior, leadership opens to all sorts of challenges and potential dangers. When people are left to establish their own set of behavioral parameters, it often doesn't get done.

Leadership is busy and stressful, and many organizations and leaders don't take the time to think about these things. Yet, the lack of expectations can shipwreck even the best of people and the best of missions.

MY STORY: WHAT WE DID

REFLECTING

I remain brokenhearted over the pain caused by such long-term abuse taking place in the environment where I served.

As I considered the history of this, I realized the church had a series of problems that blinded us to what was happening with Keith and some of the issues he created. When my wife and I started attending the church, we had no awareness of any concerns.

When I came into leadership, we were immediately addressing issues that demanded focus and attention: issues with building committee leadership, a situation with a former pastor who had embezzled, many staff departures over a short period of time, and the global pandemic. It is no wonder we didn't see it; the waters were muddy already.

One of my deepest desires is for Keith to bear the legal consequences of his choices, be held accountable for his behavior and moral failure, and for his options to be limited in the future so no other person or organization can be harmed by his narcissistic and perverse behavior. He already has received the consequences of his actions from the denominational district leadership.

It is one of my deepest desires to see the system of the church changed in a way that prevents abuse of any kind from continuing unchecked, as it did in this case. I hope the leaders, family, and friends closest to the situation will personally grapple with their role and voice, learning new ways to apply accountability and significant consequences before this could happen again.

I pray for God to redeem this season and those involved so that God may be glorified as a result.

Personally, I have come to realize that while there are many causes for discouragement in all this, I have several *major* disappointments that will require time and effort to overcome.

First, I never imagined any of Keith's actions could be abusive or sexual in nature, and it was a deeply felt shock to be confronted with the scale and scope of his actions and the impact they had on so many people in the church, his family, the district, and at the college where he taught part-time.

I knew he was troubled, but the magnitude of the abuse and damage he caused was unbelievable. And yet, I also found all this believable, since I knew what he was capable of.

Second, to my complete surprise, the church leadership (formal and informal) and members of the congregation showed a lack of grace and understanding during this situation. In addition, there was so much impatience for the biblical process to take place, which resulted in some troubling actions and demands.

I had expected more from this group of people, and I knew they could do better, but they were choosing not to. What astounded me was the lack of respect for measured responses and authority, displayed so strongly in the leadership and their spouses. While we were all wounded and frustrated, several acted poorly and without care for all those involved.

It was disturbing to discover that members of leadership were passing confidential information to one of the women, feeling that leadership wasn't doing enough and they needed to act on their own. They were working from flawed and incomplete information, acting out of frustration and not for the good of the situation or those involved. Good intentions aside, their actions didn't help and caused further damage.

Keith didn't just assault the two women (we don't know if there are others; statistically, there likely are) or even the ones he approached but who were not subject to an assault. He also abused his family, community, church members, leadership teams of elders and staff, and leadership's families. And he used and abused me, and I didn't see it.

None of us put the incidents or clues together to see what was happening. Maybe we didn't want to see it, or maybe we just didn't know what we were seeing.

Keith's widespread pattern of abuse over many years seems to have diminished in memory. This was not an isolated moment of weakness; it was a sinful pattern over a long period of time.

We need to learn from this season. Grace and understanding could have been our standard, in Christlike love, but instead, we questioned and attacked each other.

Instead, we threatened and acted out with each other.

Instead, we talked sideways to others rather than following scriptural processes.

Instead, we listened to lies rather than sought the truth.

Instead, we expected the worst from people rather than the best.

Bad behavior led to unhealthy reactions rather than spiritual and biblical responses.

OUR ACTIONS

We didn't do anything in a vacuum, nor did we make any decisions alone; there were always two or more involved in determining any action steps.

We wanted to tell everything when we first started to hear details of what happened, but we were discouraged from doing so on the advice of the police, legal counsel, and expert consultants who had been through this before. They were right to advise this.

We wanted to tell everything again after several months, when more and more came to light, and we were again discouraged because of the threats of litigation and the legal process taking place with the county attorney.

At no time did we ever think about actions to protect Keith or the reputation of the church. While we didn't want to be brutal or intentionally cause harm, we hoped to allow denominational discipline and the legal processes to play out before the church took—or considered taking—any formal kind of action.

Some of the details in the narrative should never be shared, except by those directly involved. At times, it seemed as though we were denying the voices of the women or denying the full truth to be known, but that was never part of our thinking or decision-making process.

As much as we believe the people who brought the accusations, we also needed to verify and consider what we were hearing to make sure we were acting on facts and not reacting to feelings or perceptions. This is a difficult line to walk, especially when obvious damage has been done. Prayerful and considerate actions were necessary, and we tried to honor that process.

The chair of the elders, and I as interim lead pastor, were

specifically accused of trying to protect Keith and the church name, denying the women access to our internal communications or decisions—again, that was not the case.

We also were accused of keeping things from the church and leadership. It was a rapidly changing situation with multiple levels of activity. We were careful with our communication, especially as we were very aware of some people working against the process, sharing incomplete and out-of-context information with the offender and women involved.

People were finding out confidential information and private communications, and we had no way to discern how at the time, so we erred on the side of discretion.

There were a few who suggested we didn't speak out because we were trying to be nice and avoid trouble. This was not true. We did seek a measured and prayerful response to avoid more damage by sharing the details of what we knew. If we had spoken too much too soon, experienced advisors believed the congregation might have "blown apart," or even worse, broken into splinter groups and inflicted unresolved pain on other churches.

While not overly concerned about protecting the reputation of the church or Keith, we were keenly concerned about the community of wounded people who could needlessly suffer with all the information shared.

Yes, we did have an agenda: to be responsive rather than reactive, prayerful rather than hasty, and to represent Jesus as much as we could to those who were hurt and those who had sinned. It was our concern to bring the gospel to bear on all points of this painful experience, and for love and justice to be evident.

At several points, anything we did or didn't do and anything we said or didn't say were twisted and/or called into question by the wounded, by the offender, by their agents, and even sometimes by others in leadership. All of this while we were personally brokenhearted over the pain and hardship being carried by the women and this community of believers.

I was at odds with some of the leadership at multiple points and blamed without regard for the complexity of the situation. Through it all, those leaders continued to show a lack of understanding. I didn't have time or energy to pursue long talks with each leader to ensure full understanding of all that was going on, answer all their questions, keep track of which leader said what thing to whom and when, or any number of other situational issues.

No, we were wrestling with multiple levels of conflict, multiple groups of people, and dealing with the wounds and anger of multiple women.

GOOD FROM THE BAD

We worked to put several larger and more substantive elements in place, hopefully to lay the groundwork for awareness, healing, and progress in the season ahead.

We had new elders coming on the board, but at the loss of some good men who tried to serve well and who were wounded in the process. After years of unsuccessful efforts, we finally defined the role of eldership, which could be the foundation for action items in ministry for these men as spiritual leaders and shepherds of this flock.

We activated new ministry teams, involving more of the congregation, so that decisions wouldn't be made by only a few members of leadership.

We sold some church property, which enabled us to have the financial resources for not only the pastoral search but also interim consulting and any temporary drop in giving because of this season.

We hired a team of consultants to help us navigate this interim period and into the future, and we renewed our relationship with the denomination and the district superintendent.

We provided as much support to hurting people as we could, not only with regular communication and updates but also with funds for counseling. We offered counseling to those approached but not abused, to Keith's family, and to anyone else in the congregation who was affected by all of this.

CHAPTER SIX
IN THE MIDST OF THE FIGHT

This chapter is co-written by the author, Robert Damon, and his son, Bradley Damon, who have both experienced narcissism in leadership of different organizations over many years. Through those situations, they learned skills to cope with dysfunctional and narcissistic behaviors, helped each other through those difficult seasons, and now have a strong desire to help others avoid going through similar situations. Robert is a retired pastor who also serves in various nonprofit organizations, both faith-based and community groups. Bradley is the director of a Christian wilderness camp and is involved in various nonprofit organizations, both faith-based and community groups.

Working with a narcissist can be challenging, but having a narcissist leader or boss is a challenging situation that requires some unique survival skills. In this section, we encourage responses rather than reactions, which may help anyone navigate daily life during the narcissistic battle.

In many ways, these skills can help you keep a positive

mental health balance in almost any challenging situation. In management circles, this is called self-leadership; in counseling circles, this is called self-care. In most of life, this is called positive mental health.

We defined narcissism earlier in this book, but certain realities can only be understood by actually encountering a narcissist in the workplace. In general terms, the narcissistic leader can manifest the following:

- The narcissist will take the credit others deserve, whether or not they did something right.
- The narcissist will cast blame on others, whether or not they did something wrong.
- When the narcissist is "done" with someone—and they will be at some point—the narcissist will actively work to see the person fired or pushed to resign. This action can be overt or covert in nature.
- The narcissist will exaggerate and even lie to get ahead or be seen as "better," and he or she will exaggerate and even lie to diminish someone else. It is often phrased using an "us" vs. "them" language and approach.
- The narcissist is competitive, in both big and small things, and wants to be seen as "the best."
- The narcissist will gossip with anyone who will listen; when confronted, the narcissist will deny it or claim he or she was misunderstood.
- The narcissist will pressure people to do what they normally would not, whether it is to agree with opinions, take sides based on "fuzzy" facts, or act out against someone whom the narcissist defines as troublesome.
- The narcissist will make people question their

sanity, what they believe is true, and what people think and feel.
- The narcissist will find creative and often destructive ways to diminish others to elevate him or herself.
- The narcissist will appear nice and friendly, even going out of his or her way to show support and care, until they no longer feel people are willing to feed their need for attention (narcissist supply). When the supply of attention is removed, the narcissist no longer finds value in that person and will search for new people to nurture. And that change of feelings toward others may happen over weeks, days, and sometimes even in an instant.

Those who work alongside a narcissist are reading this list and mentally checking each item, "Yes, that's true." Others may be thinking, "Oh, it can't be like this," especially in a nonprofit or faith-based organization. Both Robert and Bradley can bear testimony to this point: Yes, it's possible, and yes, it's reality.

Robert had a supervisor in a professional setting who almost fired him, observing that Robert was nodding his head when other people were talking but not when the supervisor was talking. He demanded that Robert nod his head in meetings when the supervisor was talking, showing his agreement with the supervisor to the others in the room and affirming the accuracy of what he was saying. If Robert was unable to do that, the supervisor said that he was not a team player and might fit better in another position in the organization.

Bradley found himself in a situation where the organization, and indeed the industry at large, created a distorted sense of what is expected from an employee.

Bradley's supervisor asked for an extreme level of personal sacrifice, often questioning his dedication and loyalty. Yet, the supervisor would not be subjected to any kind of scrutiny or accountability.

The organization had policies in place for reporting and accountability, but those policies were only perfunctory, and everything said and done made it clear that policies didn't matter. As a young professional learning from older and more experienced professionals in the field, Bradley found it easy to accept what he saw as normal. But when considered from a reasonable perspective, some of these expectations were not normal or acceptable.

Breaking dysfunctional patterns (or organizational culture) often comes slowly. For Bradley and Robert, one of the most important factors to precipitate a change in perspective is being involved in other communities, as well as having friends and family who are *not* associated with the organization.

For Robert, it's having coffee or lunch with other leaders who are not part of the organization, discussing situations and ideas together in a safe and positive environment.

For Bradley, participating in local theater productions is great therapy and a way to discuss experiences with a group of people who know him well and are not afraid to express their opinions.

On one occasion, while chatting backstage at a theater performance with some of the other actors, all of whom have their own day jobs in various fields outside of the theater, Bradley was sharing about his week, daily tasks, and some of the interactions he had with his supervisor. He was surprised to glance around and see looks of shock and incredulity on the faces of his friends.

He had been reflecting on what was, *to him*, a standard week—nothing extraordinary or shocking. Bradley had gotten used to it, as people often do—the frog in the kettle experience of many. It took many different and concerned voices of friends saying, "This is not normal," for him to finally reset to realistic expectations.

At one time in a nonprofit position, it was Bradley's responsibility to complete a weekly calendar, defining schedules, and assignments. Initially, Bradley did the job the way it had been done for decades: by hand, using a 3x4-foot poster with grid lines.

After several weeks, having previous experience with team scheduling, Bradley came up with another option: electronic spreadsheets, printed and posted. When suggesting the idea and advantages to his supervisor, the response was surprisingly intense. Bradley's supervisor forbade him from talking further about it, saying he still had a lot to learn about doing his job and clearly didn't have his priorities straight.

Then, with vigor, the supervisor accused Bradley of conspiring with the other staff against him, since Bradley had asked a few other staff what they thought of the idea before pitching it to the supervisor.

Having worked as supervisors, both Robert and Bradley knew how frustrating it could be when employees wanted to try something new. However, when the response to a new idea involves accusations of insubordination, insults, and suspicions of disloyalty, there's probably more going on, and it is not a trust-building experience.

In Bradley's case, keeping the calendar manually allowed his supervisor to exercise control over the staff, forcing them to operate in a space only the supervisor controlled.

There are several things needed to adjust expectations when working with or for a narcissist. Most fall within the parameters of healthy boundaries but when our guard is down, expectations met and unmet will often cause broken hearts and dashed hopes, which can sour the workplace. For instance:

- *Don't expect fairness.* There is no "fair" when dealing with a narcissist.
- *Don't expect loyalty.* The narcissist can't give it. If he or she does, it's short-term.
- *Don't expect to fix the narcissist,* no matter how much care they offer or how good people try to be around them.
- *Don't take things too personally.* The narcissist works from a created reality that is built on a world circling them; they will say the most hurtful things, which, to the narcissist, is true based on their perceived reality.
- *Don't expect credit for good work,* but do expect blame when things don't go well. If receiving any credit, it is often given in private, whereas blame is normally given in public or in small groups of people.
- *Don't believe what you hear from a narcissist.* They may say exactly what people hope to hear, or they may say something that sounds so bizarre that it seems unbelievable. The narcissist knows what will make people smile and what will make them mad or defensive, and they will play on those emotions to feed their perceived reality.
- *Don't try to explain or excuse anything* said or done, anything not said or not done, or anything someone else said or did.
- *Don't talk to other coworkers about feelings related to the narcissist.* It is helpful to find some confidants and truth tellers to help process and recover from bad days, but those people should

not be coworkers. People talk, the narcissist will hear it, and it will not go well.
- *Don't give up on yourself and your value*, and don't be afraid to make a change if needed. Whether that is finding a different department in the organization or finding an entirely new organization, trust your gut feeling and make the change.

In her article "Six Keys to Dealing with Narcissistic People," Dr. Deborah Davis writes, "Needless to say, when a person has most or all of these tendencies, you will find it difficult to connect, speak your mind, or cultivate a harmonious relationship with them. Especially if you regularly spend time together, you likely feel off balance and drained of energy, confidence, and patience in their presence."[1]

Davis highlights six ways we can equip ourselves for dealing with narcissistic people: "do not offer a diagnosis," "maintain healthy boundaries," "set clear limits," "de-escalate tension," "maintain your own dignity and self-worth," and "spend time with people who are supportive and interested in getting to know you."[2]

Robert and Bradley have developed their own list of survival techniques, which guide them in situations around narcissists but also in general leadership settings when interacting with staff, volunteers, and donors.

---

1. Deborah Davis, "Six Keys to Dealing with Narcissistic People," *Laugh, Cry, Live* (blog), *Psychology Today*, updated March 29, 2024, https://www.psychologytoday.com/us/blog/laugh-cry-live/202212/6-keys-to-dealing-with-narcissistic-people.
2. Ibid.

Be educated about narcissism

Our culture is creating more people who demonstrate narcissistic tendencies, and leaders must be aware of narcissistic behaviors and how to deal with them. Being armed with knowledge and awareness of narcissistic traits is helpful for the battle; it is important to discern if someone is being a dominant narcissist or a passive-aggressive narcissist.

In the struggle to survive and thrive in an environment with a narcissist, it is vital to remember what is really going on, especially when people start to feel sorry for the person who is behaving in narcissistic ways. Human nature is to forget what is happening, drift from the center, and excuse troubling behaviors—because we care about people, and we care about the mission. We must remember what we are facing and never let our guard down.

For those in a faith-based setting, it is not just a struggle with the bad behavior but also a battle with Satan and his agents, who are enhancing and exaggerating the bad behavior to further attack the work of God's kingdom.

It is important to separate the bad behavior from the person manifesting it, i.e., "hate the sin, love the sinner." Too often, however, organizations will ignore the long pattern of sin for the sake of the sinner, which is not biblical or healthy.

Manage your expectations

Everyone carries expectations for the day, events, and relationships, some of which are good, and some of which are not. Be careful to avoid disappointments based on unreasonable expectations and desires for outcomes or responses that the narcissist is unable to offer. For example, when you're doing a good job, don't expect to hear about it. Don't let emotions be driven by the hope for normal behavior in an abnormal environment.

Avoid triggers

Worded a bit differently, try to minimize potential points of conflict. This is *not* to say avoid conflict at any cost, but don't invite it.

Narcissists feed on drama and chaos and, while denying it, they will work hard to create conflict, only then to be seen as the fixer and "white knight" swooping in to save the day. When drama or conflict happens, stay calm and offer reasoned approaches. Or sometimes, the best thing to do is to keep a low profile and stay quiet.

Both Robert and Bradley have been told they are calming in stressful situations, in part to help de-escalate things, but also to help see things through. This works wonders when dealing with narcissists, who often seem unable to deal with calm, which can frustrate the narcissist and initiate even more negative behavior.

That said, don't fight with a narcissist. There is no "winning." It will escalate, it will hurt, and it will damage the organizational environment. It may be tempting to fight, but don't do it; the cost in emotional and tangible ways will be significant.

Good leadership behavior involves being responsive, which is ultimately stronger than being reactive. Robert has said many times to people with demanding tendencies that if an answer is needed right now, the answer is no; but with a moment to consider options and ideas, the answer may well be yes.

Obviously, taking time to respond when there is an obvious immediacy involved isn't always the best option, but more often than not, the demands for immediate action are not as urgent as people imagine. Narcissists often demand a "right now" reaction because it feeds the chaos and draws attention.

Be professional and become self-aware

Know your own personal triggers and feelings, practice good self-care, and carry yourself in a professional manner. Be careful to avoid sharing feelings, opinions, or personal information with the narcissist, as they will remember it, twist it, and use it as a weapon.

"Self-aware" sounds like a touchy-feely term. It's not all that complex. It is knowing when the feelings of frustration, anger, hurt, etc. start to build up and how to manage those feelings by removing yourself from a situation and stepping back for a moment. Do whatever will help, such as going for a walk, but learn to do whatever will help process emotions in healthy ways.

Find opportunities to self-reflect on your abilities, strengths, and weaknesses so that, when encountering narcissistic behavior and wondering what to do about it, you know what options, abilities, and resources are available to you.

When doing any type of self-inventory, have a trusted friend with you to clarify thoughts and ideas and provide a different perspective as you look at some potentially difficult truths.

Regarding self-awareness, don't be shy about owning your strengths. Asserting them in a healthy way may defuse a situation, if only for a moment. Likewise, there is no shame in claiming weaknesses and shortcomings either. This is a beautiful truth: Anyone is capable of accomplishing things despite, and sometimes even because of, their vulnerabilities.

When going into difficult situations with knowledge of personal strengths and abilities, it may be that the only option available is to disengage before being destroyed by narcissistic behavior. At other times, you may discover the strength to persevere through a particular set of circumstances and maintain boundaries for some time despite a barrage of narcissistic behavior and attacks.

In personal and professional settings, self-awareness is important in deciding whether it is better to stay in a long-term situation (job, relationship, organization, location, etc.), remove yourself from that situation, or effect some kind of change to the situation to make it sustainable.

Consider all the factors and decide how to survive and even, dare we say, thrive under the circumstances.

Establish boundaries

Take time to think about boundaries, and consider what is too much, too far, and personal limits. *Then,* the real challenge— hold to it! Validate and affirm the narcissistic boss or supervisor, when possible, without betraying self-integrity or confidence.

Notice and affirm good behaviors, but call out the negative ones.

Robert had a time when those limits were tested by a narcissist. However, he had taken time to think about his role in the organization and why it mattered. Because he knew his limits and his "why," Robert was able to bring a more reasonable approach to those difficult situations in which he was pushed.

But the time came when being truthful to the moment was no longer effective, the fight was becoming too much, and the only response was to leave the organization. Only the narcissist boss and the leadership board knew the real reasons, but the organization continued, and the narcissist was eventually held accountable, no longer with that organization.

Document everything

Note everything. Take notes on meetings with dates, discussions, times, action items, and decisions made. After meetings, restate discussion points, action items, and decisions in an email to the people in the meeting and the narcissist leader.

It may also be helpful to document private discussions and statements to track what was said and details that need to be remembered.

At one point in Robert's career, working for a nonprofit that partnered with other organizations, he and his organization's leadership made a critical decision that resulted in a very public crisis for one of the other organizations; in fact, it shut them down. The leaders of that organization took legal action against Robert and the nonprofit he represented, with a significant financial outcome, and lots of media and drama were involved. But Robert had excellent documentation of dates and actions, with a binder of operating procedures and two specific emails that were follow-ups to face-to-face meetings, all of which became deciding factors to resolve the case in Robert's favor.

Develop rewarding activities outside of the narcissist's circle

Rest, exercise, develop a hobby, and spend time with people who refresh you. For the narcissist leader, there are no boundaries between work and home, and time dedicated to work, home, or family starts to become unbalanced and conflicted.

As a non-narcissist, it is vital to protect and guard your balance and to be careful not to allow the narcissist to invade and fragment time dedicated to your spouse, family, home, and interests.

Robert developed a hobby working with stained glass, and he started to volunteer at a local community organization. Those times created moments when the drama and chaos of the narcissistic environment were not front and center in his mind. In fact, it created more opportunities to express his personal skills and gifts in ways that deeply encouraged him.

Plus, Robert keeps a small group of men close in daily life that he meets with weekly for coffee and discussion.

Bradley continues acting in local theater groups, makes sure to go camping a couple of times a year with non-work friends, and plays board games once a week with a group of non-work friends. He also is connected with a small group that meets each Thursday morning at a local restaurant.

Avoid being alone with a narcissist

This is challenging to accomplish at times, and there are moments when being one-on-one with a narcissist cannot be avoided. But try to draw in others so the chaos and drama are limited, and there are witnesses to what is said and any decisions made.

In Robert's experience, this only frustrated the narcissist and often began the process of changing boundaries and limits. Over time, their desire to interact diminished.

For Bradley, the worst moments always came when he was one-on-one with a narcissist. That's when the narcissist's mask would slip, and the snarling would start.

The silver lining is that, in cases where Bradley followed the survival strategies in this book, those intense moments caused the narcissists to become more desperate for control, eventually leading them to expose themselves to rebuke from their organizations.

Once the narcissists try to intimidate others and are met with healthy boundaries, they find themselves in a scary situation, where someone honest and straightforward sees the narcissist for who they are and is neither intimidated nor moved to rash actions. Outlasting a narcissist is usually easier than out-matching them.

Speak the truth

With appropriate boundaries and limits in place, it's safe to speak the truth, saying, "That's not OK," or "That's not true." When getting thrown under the bus, calmly speak back the truth to the untruth, using respect and positive language as much as possible.

It can be useful to avoid accusing the boss of wrongdoing or error, and it may escalate to saying he or she is wrong. Calmly say, "To clarify, it was . . ." this or that. Speak the truth, document the moment, and keep moving.

Bradley experienced a teacher behaving narcissistically in a classroom where he was working as a paraprofessional. The class was a group of students with autism. This teacher was mercifully only in the classroom for a couple of hours each week, but it was incredibly destructive nonetheless, because she always was more focused on proving her superior intelligence than she was on educating the students.

The teacher would give faulty teaching examples and blame the students for their failure to apply the examples. When the students would rephrase a concept accurately, she would tell them they were wrong and correct them by using slightly different words but saying the same thing.

When students pointed out her errors, the teacher would tell them they clearly didn't understand the material; when Bradley pointed out her errors, this teacher lodged a formal complaint with his supervisor. Luckily, the supervisor knew this teacher and Bradley well enough, and the complaints never progressed.

While Bradley never launched any complaints against her, the teacher did not return the following year. This is why, when dealing with a narcissist, your survival is more important than competing with them. With integrity and patience, you are more likely to outlast them than you are to beat them at their own game.

Robert was meeting with the human resources manager in an organization, discussing some staffing issues and determining options, and the director of the organization (who was very narcissistic) was irritated that they were meeting without her. She paced outside the full-glass office door and made her presence known.

While Robert focused on the meeting, the director behaved more aggressively. Finally, she burst into the room and said, "Good, I'm glad you are both here. I need to talk to you both about something."

Robert responded simply, "Obviously, your issue is more

important than ours, so what do you need?" She paused, looked at Robert, and kept going. Speaking truth into the moment let the director know a boundary was crossed, but Robert didn't engage in battle over the offense.

You are *not* alone

It is vital to have a trusted advisor outside of the circle of the narcissist to vent and hear feedback. As always, talk to the human resources representative if needed. (Note: If the organization is too small for an identified HR person, find someone on the board leadership who would take a concern.) There is always *someone* to speak to within the organization about any concerns, but if there isn't, it is an unstable environment, and a change of some kind should be considered.

Additionally, have a truth-teller or two in life. It might be a spouse, a close friend, or a mentor. Either way, it should be someone who can speak back, be caring in their feedback, and offer support when needed. Remind yourself of your value, no matter what the narcissist is saying.

Self-care is a consistent theme in managing life with narcissistic people. In some cases, you can distance yourself from the impact of people with narcissistic tendencies, but for many in work or family situations when distance is not an option, practicing self-care, especially having healthy boundaries, is a critical skill.

During a battle that involves drama, chaos, and perceived realities, being healthy in your physical, mental, spiritual, and emotional center is necessary. Learn whatever skills possible to find balance and calm. Walk, work out, practice an artistic hobby, listen to music, etc.—whatever it takes.

For faith-based leadership, it remains necessary to ground our thinking in scripture, to remind one another of what the mission and goal really are and how leaders should carry themselves.

While we could cite many Bible passages, several basic sections define leadership in clear, easy-to-understand terms: 1 Timothy 3:1–13; Titus 1:5–16; 1 Peter 5:1–11; and Ezekiel 34. These passages have been helpful for Robert over many years to understand what good leadership is, especially when faced with bad leadership and narcissistic people.

Yes, there are other verses. Specifically, for this study, consider also the truths in Colossians 3:5–14 and Galatians 5:19–26. Look for leaders who exemplify this pattern of living and for the echoes of their work and presence to see what is being exhibited in their leadership and relationships.

- Leaders should *not* exhibit sexual immorality, impurity, debauchery, lust, evil desires, greed, envy, anger, malice, rage, slander, filthy language, lying, idolatry, witchcraft, hatred, discord, dissensions, jealousy, and selfish ambitions.
- Leaders *should* exhibit compassion, kindness, humility, gentleness, patience, unity (bearing with one another), forgiveness, love, peace, thankfulness, joy, goodness, and self-control.

If any of the former list is present and being manifested in even the slightest way, there is a need to pause and seek prayerful assistance. We should take note of the difference between a one-time experience and a chronic pattern over an extended period of time.

Mistakes, miscommunications, and misunderstandings are common when people work side-by-side, so it's important to look for patterns in people's behavior, whether positive or negative.

Without question, if any of the latter list is present, there is a need to celebrate and continue forward. If you look closely enough, these patterns and outcomes will become obvious, and it will help any leader to define the need to "fight, flight, or flounder."

MY STORY: THE EPILOGUE

Some might wonder if I have lost my love of the church. *I have not.* The church remains the beautiful bride of Christ, and it is a community created by God, moderated by the love of Christ, working through the Holy Spirit. It is a group of flawed and damaged people, redeemed by Christ and guided by the Spirit of God. I love the church; if anything, I love the ideal of the church community even more than before.

Some might wonder if I have lost my love for pastoral ministry. *I have not.* Many in our culture believe serving as a pastor is only for those who can do nothing else, or for those who are somehow mentally unbalanced or weak-minded. I believe serving in pastoral ministry is not for the faint of heart or weak in spirit.

In truth, pastoral ministry is for those who *cannot not* do it (double negative intended); this is often referred to as a "calling." The work of God through the community of the church is *the most significant* endeavor on the face of the planet, building up the Body of Christ (the Church). Being part of that as a pastor is an amazing honor and responsibility.

After months of serving as interim lead pastor, many prayerful discussions with God and several long discussions with my wife, I felt God was leading me to step back from my role for the arrival of an outside interim pastor with experience in situations like this, working with a team of advisors who could help shape the direction of the congregation going forward.

I did not give up or give in, and I did not leave because of any appeal by church members or leadership for me to do so. God is the one who called me to step into all of this, and God is the one who clearly said it was time to step out.

The congregation has moved forward with a renewed mission. The church has hired a permanent lead pastor, and the community seems to be thriving.

Over the last years, multiple people have approached me (and the former chair of the board and other leaders) to apologize for their behavior and/or express their appreciation for the hard work we did during that whole season. It is humbling and restorative, and these actions reflect God's grace in great measure.

God was not surprised by all of this, and He is not a passive observer as people recover and experience healing.

Personal healing and recovery from what happened continues, but God is working through a lot of pain to bring restoration and hope. My sense of place and serving in the church still seems elusive, but I am benefiting from a season of rest.

The ministry immediately before me is prayer, encouragement, and speaking into moments when invited. I may be retired from a full-time pastoral location, but my journey seems far from done.

I share all of this with no desire to make me sound like the hero of my own story. Far from it. This is not an attempt to defend or justify my actions. I must reiterate that this narrative is my reflection and not necessarily meant to be an exact or detailed documentation of all that happened. Likely, I have missed some details, and there was much I didn't know at the time, or since.

I didn't anticipate a season like this. No one does, and no one in their right mind would hope for this kind of experience.

It's ironic, but I never aspired to serve as a lead pastor. Ever. I still don't. Faithful is all I wanted to be, to do more good than harm, and to leave whatever I touched in better shape than how I found it.

CHAPTER SEVEN
RECOMMENDED PLAN OF ACTION

As a result of this learning and experience, I would recommend the following plan of action *as strongly as I can*.

First, leaders, staff, board members, volunteer leaders, and, if possible, representatives from the organization's membership must talk through these concepts. They must communicate about appropriate boundaries, expectations of behavior, and levels of accountability and authority that provide a sense of safety and meaning. Tangible measures must be in place to provide adequate boundaries and accountability. Don't just give lip service to this discussion; make it real.

Review policy. The team must take a long look at their policy handbook. If a handbook is not in use, the team must collaborate to create one. Use HR experts from the organization to help, and contact the district leadership for additional assistance as needed. As policy and best practices are evolving, any examples included here would be quickly outdated.

Review basic understandings of conduct. If there are

no expectations of appropriate conduct in place, the team needs to write a code of conduct that fits the context. There are plenty of examples to draw from, including several listed in Appendix B. Having real parameters of conduct is vital for effective leadership.

Implement a clear structure of accountability and authority, and include responsibilities and tangible consequences of both success and failure. Having this defined will also help with evaluations.

There is a strong need to apply a guiding structure in such a way that provides safety and context without squashing the dynamic leadership methods and unique community of the faith-based environment in a congregation or nonprofit organization.

Develop a process and tools for annual reviews for staff and leadership, not just subjective to how people feel, but an objective measure of progress and areas for improvement. This needs to be a safe process that does not become punitive in nature. The denominational district leadership can assist as needed.

As a leader who has worked in both nonprofit and for-profit settings, please hear my plea: make evaluations meaningful, based not on subjective feelings of any one person but on objective measures founded on role descriptions and organizational needs. In faith-based settings, those objective measures can be more dynamic and fluid in nature, but objective evaluations are still possible and needed.

Include the staff and board together in this process of discovery about conduct, policies, and evaluations, discovering what could work and making it happen. Consider involving leadership members' spouses as well, and allow them to have a voice in this process that affects them.

***Ask for help* as needed.** Don't be afraid of this. Ask the experts who are business leaders, but also ask denominational district leadership for help.

Further research is essential in this area of leadership. There is a profound absence of discussion and adequate study on the prevention of clergy abuse and dysfunctional behavior, especially in the emerging post-pandemic environment.

The recent widespread and public issues within the Catholic church and the Southern Baptist Convention have both skewed the data and discussion significantly. As I have come to find, there are few—if any—studies on evangelical pastoral behaviors and abuse, and we need some aspiring PhD students to take up the slack and do the work.

We need researchers to consider leadership, power differentials, hubris, and abuse, and for that research to inform some metric that would add definition to leaders and organizations struggling to understand this issue of narcissism in leadership.

Dr. Wilder comments on this in his extensive work on spirituality in the church community. In *The Other Half of Church*, he writes, "Some scholars are attempting to measure the prevalence of narcissism in Christian leadership but have yet to agree on the proper measurement instruments. We will have to wait for new studies before we can quantify the extent and depth of narcissism in the pastorate."[1]

And last, cover this whole process in prayer, grace, tact, and humor at every level. Yes, humor—at least as much as can be mustered while discussing all of this. This will take time to implement and make personal, but it is worth the effort, and the results will benefit the ministry.

Grace and tact are scarce in our culture, whether in

---

1. E. James Wilder and Michael Hendricks, *The Other Half of the Church: Christian Community, Brain Science, and Overcoming Spiritual Stagnation* (Chicago: Moody Publishers, 2020), 165.

business, politics, or social settings. May that *never* be true when talking about faith-based leadership, and may our informed leadership be a benchmark for others coming behind us to face successes and challenges with humor, grace, and tact.

APPENDIX A: TOOLS, IN DETAIL

The following is recommended for leadership on every level of an organization. These *highly* encouraged recommendations will help prevent the abuse of power and position.

Accountability and Boundaries

Define meaningful points of accountability, with consequences for success and failure. Accountability need not be punitive in nature but *developmental* and *affirming*. Some boundaries are set *for* the person, and some are set *by* the person.

Overall, it is the reality that no one is acting or allowed to act on their own. And these should be reviewed regularly, at least annually, potentially as part of an evaluation process.

- **Time**: balance between personal and professional, work, and home, establishing a structure and schedule to do everything possible to fully work and fully relax.

- **Financial**: define any concerns with finances—professional and personal.
- **Relationships**: establish a close circle of people who are not afraid to verify how relationships are managed at work and home, defining any conflicts or challenges that remain unresolved.
- **Technology**: define points of balance and purity, including time use.
- **Education**: list and plan any goals or expectations on learning, including when and how it may be funded.
- **Spirituality**: refine routines and schedules to ensure spiritual nourishment, especially in ways that are not based on position or responsibilities.
- **Random**: discover what areas of support and help are most needed.

Once a point of accountability or boundaries is identified, place some markers in place to check on health and progress—progressive in nature depending on success or challenge.

Again, the whole point of accountability is developmental and affirming. If it is intended to be punitive, or as documentation toward discipline or termination, it moves from accountability to a performance improvement plan, which is a whole different matter.

Mentoring Relationships

The more responsibilities and visibility of a role, the more vital the need. Ideally, at least one person "above" (semi-annually), at least one person "behind" (monthly), and at least one person "alongside" (weekly). The key to mentoring is asking open questions, rather than the easier closed questions. This type of role can be referred to as "mentoring discipleship."

Mentoring is an overused term, and, in this culture, more people are seeking to be mentored than agreeing to mentor other people. Our experience and culture have made serving as a mentor appear almost overwhelming and something that requires a whole set of attitudes and knowledge. But in the culture of faith and community, mentoring doesn't need to be as scary as it first seems. Mentoring and being mentored is simply being alongside one another as a friend and encourager, to bring out the best in people, but also remind the mentee of who they really are in Christ. And in that process, both mentor and mentee benefit.

It is critical that at least three levels of mentoring relationships be part of any faith-based leader's routine, especially in senior leadership roles.

First, *meet regularly with someone who is "above" the mentee*, whether that is someone in a specific leadership role or someone more mature/experienced. It's a person who can speak to moments of confusion and fear, coaching good thinking and right actions. Ideally, this could be a quarterly time to talk, via face-to-face conversation, phone call, or video chat. At the very least, semi-annual meetings are necessary for effective mentoring.

Second, *meet monthly with someone who is "behind" the mentee*, to build into their life and hear the good ideas in their thinking. As we speak into each other's lives, we are speaking into our own. That person can ask any questions, bring any concerns, and offer any thoughts—with the expectation of dialogue around the topic in the safety of a good relationship.

At times, this is a fun adventure, and at other times, it is a painful time of correction and insight. But it is vital to build into someone who is growing in life and leadership, in the safety of an affirming and encouraging setting.

Lastly, *meet weekly with someone who is alongside as a peer*, a good friend who can tell if you are faking life or dodging issues. This kind of relationship happens over a longer period of time—that person (ideally, they become a good friend) checks on the other person and is close enough to see how they're living. These friends might ask questions that are often hard to hear.

It is difficult work to find these levels of relationship, especially for key and visible leaders, and it takes time and effort. I have sought one or two people who are "above" me in my life and role to speak into me with words of correction and encouragement.

I have also sought to build a circle of two or three guys who are seeing me and talking with me weekly and know me and my spouse well. They know when I am hurting, and they can call out the flaws in my self-justifying thoughts.

Last, I have humbly sought to relationally invest in people who specifically ask for it, whether for a short period of time or over a longer time. I am careful not to overextend these commitments, because they *do* take time to nurture, and it is a delight to pray for and encourage a group of people who are in leadership roles. So far, they seem to appreciate the relationship and contacts we have.

It is vital to develop a new understanding of what mentoring means and work to build formal or casual relationships that will help not only in the current setting but also into the future.

Continuing Education

Many other careers require some form of continuing education, especially when these are positions of responsibility, trust, and power. It has long baffled me why pastoral or faith-based leadership is not required to participate in continuing education, no matter the status of titles or education.

In the setting of faith-based leadership and pastoral roles, the potential topics that should be required are vast: abuse prevention, safety in the community, use of power, aspects of grace, lessons on grief and forgiveness, healthy evaluation/assessment, managing stress, financial integrity, personal family health, etc.

Maybe continuing education is required as onsite or online seminars, reading books, or logging into a discussion, etc. In this current culture, resources and thinking about some of these topics are changing fast, and it is important to stay current. Continuing education topics are not just geared toward biblical knowledge or academic achievements but also toward the personal and spiritual development of the pastor or leader.

It is recommended that a specific number of hours be required. If it's not based on a denominational standard, it could be required and encouraged at the board level of specific organizations or churches. With online resources available now like no other time in history, this requirement could be managed easily. And the benefit to the local organizations and the long-term health of the faith communities is beyond measure.

Certainly, with colleges offering both online and onsite courses, even for audits, this recommendation is possible to integrate easily.

Check-Ins with Key Relationships

For any leader, regular check-ins are needed with spouse and children, best friends, and other staff members. Again, these contacts need not be punitive or invasive in nature but instead should be developmental and preventive.

If managing boards and supervisors would take the time to do a quick check-in with the people who are around the leaders on a more regular basis, we may be able to catch issues and celebrate successes on a much more meaningful scale.

In the business setting, this is often referred to as a "360 Review," but the scope needs to be wider, including not just those who work around this person but also those who live with them.

As recent examples have made clear, a quick check-in with the spouse or children on how things are going can prevent a catastrophic crash from destroying the family and leaving many shattered relationships.

Family members and close friends may temper their responses for any number of reasons, but one often can get a sense of what's going on by reading between the lines of what is said or unsaid.

Define Life Clues

This recommendation is more subjective than objective, but it is still important. If possible, define some life clues that may point to an issue or challenge that is at work in the leader's life. It may be the tone and words being used with family and staff, or even to the organization, that serve as a clue to stress or personal challenges. Language can serve as a clue to the start of a problem, as a careless use of words can be the start of a slide into deeper issues.

It may be the use of time, whether too much in the office or too little, too much time being invisible, and not enough time around people, or even taking too much or too little time on tasks. All serve as clues that something is amiss in the life of the leader.

There may be some life clues about moods or attitudes, how close relationships are going, or even financial clues that come up (stress over vehicle or home repairs, avoiding spending money, or spending way too much money all at once, etc.).

It is good if someone close to the leader (not family) could be attentive to those clues and ask the tough questions. After asking the questions and hearing the responses, that person has the responsibility to do something about it, such as contact the spouse or coworkers to get more information, connect with the leader's supervisor to ask for help, or even reach out to the supervising board or denominational leader to express concern and ask for help.

If the leader can think for him or herself on this topic, he or she may offer a mentor or friend some insights about what to look for and ask for help identifying. For example, I have some friends who know that when I don't look them in the eye while talking, or when I take an exceptionally quiet stance during conversations, something is not right, or I'm bothered by something I've heard.

It is much better to act proactively on these things before a major issue occurs than it is to react or respond after the fact.

Ask Key Questions

If a leader is trying to hide something from others or is playing games with behaviors, he or she will take a defensive position when asked questions on a repeated basis. However, I've found that most healthy leaders enjoy being asked and welcome the opportunity to talk less about issues of work and more about concerns of life. This is a relational piece to leadership development. Checking to see how people are doing by asking key questions about what the leader is focused on is paramount.

- How are you spending your time?
- What are you reading?

- What are your top three prayer concerns right now?
- Do you have and can you list a trusted circle of friends?
- How are you handling your finances?
- What is the first thing you do in the morning and the last thing you do at night?
- How is your marriage and family life?
- How full is your schedule?
- What issues are you experiencing within your leadership, and how are you handling it?
- What types of things do you want to do but can't find time to do?
- What are you doing to relax?
- How is your social media presence?
- What are you doing to build into the people around you?
- How are you keeping yourself pure with internet and media use?
- What are you learning about God?
- What are you learning about yourself?

Watch how the leader responds. If there is a pause, or the leader tries to dodge answering, or the leader attempts to answer and then changes the subject, these are clues to pay attention to.

These also could be questions that leadership teams or boards ask of each other regularly. These answers could be foundational to deeper relationships being formed, which can be helpful in times when strong relationships are needed to sort through a challenging season.

Annual Evaluations

Sadly, many organizations do not provide annual evaluations for their staff and leadership. In addition, many organizations do not provide role descriptions, which are foundational for evaluations but also needed for objective determinations of progress or refinement.

Evaluations provide important feedback based on personal and role-driven objectives and goals, and these can serve as markers over time to assess effective placement in the role—and in the needs of the organization as a whole.

If we are honest, we must admit that evaluations also have been used by some leaders as a tool to brow-beat and demean another person. This cannot be allowed to happen, and, when it does, action needs to be taken to limit the damage. Regular evaluations done in a safe way can be a blessing to everyone involved, and they can drive the organization and leadership to higher levels of success.

As I've seen from experience, the role of the evaluation is valid in both larger organizations and smaller ones. It provides the time to celebrate success and progress, set markers for improvement and reviews, share expectations between staff and supervisor, and highlight needs within the organization that are not covered by existing staff.

Evaluations need to be real and measurable, and they should include both role execution and spiritual development. I recommend including the board and denominational leadership as much as possible in evaluations. In some cases, leaders may wish to include a counselor to assess personal mental and spiritual health and well-being.

The most effective tactic is to define the role with specific action plans, then base the evaluation on the specific items listed in the action plan. Look for and define steps for measurable actions to take over the course of the next year or two and explain what success in that area might look like.

In the healthiest of evaluations, looking for tendencies *toward* the criteria is ideal rather than expecting people to meet *all* criteria. For many action points in faith-based leadership, success is measured in the direction or progress people make rather than the tangible numbers they meet. In faith-based goals, numbers are useful as indicators but not the full measure of progress or success.

The first action is to define a role description and then conduct an evaluation as a baseline measure with annual evaluations to assess progress. If possible, in some, if not all cases, quarterly reviews and discussions are ideal. Using a metric or rubric with clearly defined boxes for comment and action plans may be helpful.

This recommended point is to provide objective rather than subjective evaluations for people, based not so much on feelings but more on expectations and direction.

> *"You don't have to apologize for the way that our boundaries inconvenience other people. It's not your job to accommodate their wants and needs at your own expense."*
> —Michell C. Clark

APPENDIX B: CODE OF CONDUCT

The National Association of Evangelicals (NAE) has a valuable code of ethics to consider. There are multiple elements of this code, paraphrased here.

- **Pursue Integrity**:
    - in *character* by being ruthlessly honest, patient, diligent, and avoiding conflicts of interest;
    - in *personal care* (spiritual, mental, emotional, and physical); in *preaching and teaching* by speaking truth and giving credit when using words or ideas of others.
- **Be Trustworthy**:
    - in *leadership* by using power prudently and humbly, keeping promises;
    - with *information* by guarding confidences, communicating truthfully;
    - with *resources*, by being prudent with personal and ministry resources, and making sure gifts are used as intended.

- **Seek Purity**:
    - in *sexual purity* by avoiding sinful sexual behavior and inappropriate involvements, resist temptations;
    - in *spiritual formation* by seeking the help of the Holy Spirit, faithful devotion to the Lord, and being consistent in prayer and study;
    - in *theology*, by regular study of the Bible and sound doctrine; in *professional practice*, by identifying a counselor to provide counsel and advice, develop awareness of needs and vulnerability, and avoid exploitation or manipulation by any means.
- **Embrace Accountability**:
    - in *finances* by accepting accounting practices and audits and using ministry funds as intended;
    - in *ministry responsibilities* by clarity of authority structures, decision-making procedures, clarity of roles and policies, and model this at every level;
    - in *denomination or ministry organizations* by ensuring compliance with standards and expectations, including regular reporting.
- **Facilitate Fairness**:
    - with *staff* by following practices for staff selection and advocating equitable pay/benefits and providing regular staff interactions and honest feedback;
    - with *church members* by ensuring appropriate access to staff and assuming responsibility for the spiritual health of the church;
    - with *community* by building cooperation with

local ministries and providing ministry to the public;
- with *prior congregations* by not recruiting people to come with you and avoid interfering in ministry of previous congregations.[1]

Christianityworks also provides a detailed code of conduct for their staff "explicitly setting out what we do and what we don't do as a team, we have accountability and transparency before one another and before God."[2] Their recommendations are as follows.

- **Bible-based Behavior**:
    - honor God in ministry and personal life;
    - be kind, generous, loving, decent, respectful, and honest with one another;
    - declare any conflicts of interest;
    - deal honestly, ethically, and decently in all matters, including financial.
- **Financial**:
    - treat all funds as a gift from God;
    - do not make large payments or purchases on your own;
    - do not pay bribes, inducements, or incentives;
    - use funds only for mission of the ministry; keep accurate records;
    - provide regular, comprehensive, and transparent reporting to the board;
    - have a plan if anyone suspects or detects

---

1. "Code of Ethics for Pastors," National Association of Evangelicals, accessed August 3, 2025, https://www.nae.org/code-of-ethics-for-pastors/.
2. "Code of Conduct," About Christianityworks, Christianityworks, accessed August 3, 2025, https://christianityworks.com/about-christianityworks/code-of-conduct/.

financial irregularities or inappropriate expenditures;
  - ensure annual audit.
- **Supporters and Members**:
  - treat all information as confidential, and place effective measures in place to protect privacy;
  - respond to and thank all those involved in timely, honest, respectful, and loving ways.
- **Ministry Assets**:
  - make sure assets are insured and kept safe for ministry use;
  - avoid personal use of ministry assets, unless approved by CEO and/or the Board, and without causing any cost or loss to the ministry;
  - store information and data securely; document intellectual property and licensing arrangements.
- **Personal Behavior:**
  - prevent any form or harassment, bullying, demeaning behavior;
  - work through difficult situations such as performance issues or conflict by speaking truth in love and making every effort to build up one another;
  - expect mistakes and failure from time to time; do not have a blame-oriented culture but rather learn and forgive before moving on;
  - understand that dishonesty, laziness, and bad attitudes have no place in ministry;
  - expect people to work hard, bring their gifts, experience and insights to bear as part of the team, all for the glory of God.

- **Moral Behavior**:
    - Avoid being alone with a member of the opposite sex who is not a spouse or family member, in the office, working away from the office, traveling, sharing coffee or meals, etc.;
    - do not travel with team members of the opposite sex, ever;
    - provide spouse with complete access to all tech equipment and applications to ensure transparency and accountability;
    - maintain sexual purity at work and in private life, irrespective of status or position, and failure is likely to result in dismissal from ministry.[3]

Applying the Code to Difficult Decisions: In situations that could be considered difficult or dangerous, one needs to pause and consider, think about the potential, and ask for help and/or refer as needed.[4]

Reporting a Breach: No one will suffer any disadvantage for making a report of a breach, unless of course it is deliberately false or malicious; it is hoped there is never a need to report, but if there is, a report is expected, because we exist to bring glory to God and our holiness is the basis on which we serve and how God blesses this ministry.[5]

Author's note: I find the absence of spiritual expectations interesting, such as being involved in worship, active in prayer, diligent in the study of God's Word, a member of a local

---

3. Ibid.
4. Ibid.
5. Ibid.

congregation, etc. I'm not sure why this is overlooked, but I would certainly include it. Without any desire to make this a checklist to somehow attain a level of spirituality that is acceptable, which is subjective and difficult to assess, it is important to communicate that some measure of spiritual growth and nurturing is taking place in the life of a leader, especially one in a faith-based organization or congregation. All too often, we assume spirituality is a given when, in fact, it is the first hint of drift when worship, prayer, and scripture are neglected.

APPENDIX C: A FEW WORDS ON FORGIVENESS

Forgiveness is tricky business for most people, especially when holding a romanticized perspective that if forgiveness is granted, we can forget what happened and everyone can move forward believing all is right with the world. That is not reality, and it is not what is found in scripture.

A good friend and board member had a pattern of lying over a long period of time, and I ended up calling him out for the behavior and separating from the relationship and that specific leadership team. He contacted me several years later in hopes of reestablishing the friendship, since he "missed the old times." I had forgiven him and told him so, but he seemed unaware of why he would need to be forgiven. In our conversation, I reflected no ill feelings and wished him well, but told him I was not going to step back into the environment where the hurt could happen again. Forgiven, yes; forgotten, no.

Forgiveness, repentance, and restoration are challenging relational dynamics, as most people hold wildly distorted views and unrealistic hopes when something has happened, whether as the offender, the offended, or people close to one or both individuals.

My own journey through forgiveness after experiencing narcissistic abuse has been full of staggered steps, processing feelings, and reading what God has to say about it. There are volumes written about forgiveness that can do a much better job unpacking this than I could attempt here.

Other than the Bible, I recommend three excellent resources for consideration, especially if anyone is standing in the ashes of a damaged soul or working through the rubble of a congregation or nonprofit.

First, Tim Keller's book *Forgive* is an excellent study on what it means to approach forgiveness and repentance on a spiritual level. This book is structured for study by individuals or groups, and the narrative will lead the readers through a journey of discovery of the biblical definitions in this process.

Second, I recommend June Hunt's resource called *Forgiveness*, part of the larger pool of resources in the Biblical Counseling Keys series.

Lastly, in every leader's toolkit, there should be the book *Peacemaker* by Ken Sande. This is useful in spiritual or secular organizations and is available in age-appropriate versions. While not a narrative to read, it is a great resource to use.

BIBLIOGRAPHY

American Psychiatric Association. *Diagnostic and Statistical Manual of Mental Disorders, Fifth Edition.* Washington, DC: American Psychiatric Association Publishing, 2017.

Asad, Sarosh, and Eugene Sadler-Smith. "Differentiating Leader Hubris and Narcissism on the Basis of Power." *Sage Journals* 16, no. 1 (February 2020): 39-61. https://doi.org/10.1177/1742715019885763.

Ball, R. Glenn and Darrel Puls. "Frequency of Narcissistic Personality Disorder in Pastors: A Preliminary Study." Report presented to American Association of Christian Counselors, Nashville, September 26, 2015.

Christianityworks. "Code of Conduct." About Christianityworks. Accessed August 3, 2025. https://christianityworks.com/about-christianityworks/code-of-conduct/.

Davis, Deborah. "Six Keys to Dealing with Narcissistic People." *Laugh, Cry, Live* (blog). *Psychology Today,* updated March 29, 2024. https://www.psychologytoday.com/us/blog/laugh-cry-live/202212/6-keys-to-dealing-with-narcissistic-people.

DeGroat, Charles. "Finding Narcissism in Church." *The Banner.* December 28, 2020. https://www.thebanner.org/features/2020/12/finding-narcissism-in-church.

DeGroat, Charles. "Narcissistic Leadership in the Church." A Foundation for Theological Education, John Wesley Fellowship. Published on October 13, 2021.
https://johnwesleyfellows.org/perspectives/narcissistic-leadership-in-the-church/.

DeGroat, Charles. *When Narcissism Comes to Church: Healing Your Community From Emotional and Spiritual Abuse.* Downers Grove, IL: InterVarsity Press, 2020.

G.R.A.C.E. *Emotional and Spiritual Abuse.* Handout given at leadership training presentation in Saint Paul, MN, September 2023.

Kohut, Heintz. *The Analysis of the Self: A Systematic Approach to the Psychoanalytic Treatment of Narcissistic Personality Disorders.* New York: International University Press, 1976.

Keltner, Dacher. "Power Paradox." *Greater Good Magazine.* Published on December 1, 2007. https://greatergood.berkeley.edu/article/item/power_paradox.

Langberg, Diane. *Redeeming Power: Understanding Authority and Abuse in the Church.* Grand Rapids, MI: Brazos Press/Baker Publishing, 2020.

McIntosh, Gary L., and Samuel D. Rima. *Overcoming the Dark Side of Leadership: How to Become an Effective Leader by Confronting Potential Failures.* Grand Rapids: Baker Books, 2007.

National Association of Evangelicals. "Code of Ethics for Pastors." Accessed August 3, 2025. https://www.nae.org/code-of-ethics-for-pastors/.

Puls, Darrell. *Let Us Prey: The Plague of Narcissist Pastors and What We Can Do About It.* Eugene, OR: Cascade Books, 2020.

Psych DB. "Narcissistic Personality Disorder." Last modified January 27, 2024. https://www.psychdb.com/personality/narcissistic.

Psychology Today. "Narcissism." Basics. Accessed August 3, 2025. https://www.psychologytoday.com/us/basics/narcissism.

Sparks, Dana. "Narcissistic personality disorder: Inflated sense of importance." Mayo Clinic News Network. Published on September 15, 2020. https://newsnetwork.mayoclinic.org/discussion/narcissistic-personality-disorder-inflated-sense-of-importance/.

Telloian, Courtney. "5 Types of Narcissism." Psych Central. Updated on December 18, 2024. https://psychcentral.com/health/types-of-narcissism.

Tolkien, J. R. R. *Two Towers.* London: HarperCollins, 2005.

Twenge, Jean M., and W. Keith Campbell. *The Narcissism Epidemic: Living in the Age of Entitlement.* New York: Simon & Schuster/Atria, 2009.

Weitz, Kevin, and William Bergquist. "In Search of Truth I: Hubris and Narcissism." *Library of Professional Psychology.* Published on July 9,

2020. https://library.psychology.edu/in-search-of-truth-i-hubris-and-narcissism/.

Wilder, E. James, and Michel Hendricks. *The Other Half of Church: Christian Community, Brain Science, and Overcoming Spiritual Stagnation.* Chicago: Moody Publishers, 2020.

Wilder, E. James. *The Pandora Problem: Facing Narcissism in Leaders and Ourselves.* Carmel, IN: Deeper Walk International, 2018.

Williford, Craig and Carolyn. *How to Treat a Staff Infection: Resolving Problems in Your Church or Ministry.* Grand Rapids: Baker Books, 2006.

RESOURCES FOR FURTHER READING

Asamoah-Gyadu, J. Kwabena. "'Be Imitators of Me as I Am of Christ': Integrity as a Lifestyle of Christian Leaders." Published September 2024. https://lausanne.org/global-analysis/be-imitators-of-me-as-i-am-of-christ-integrity-as-a-lifestyle-of-christian-leaders.

Batchelor, Valli Boobal, ed., *When Pastors Prey: Overcoming Clergy Sexual Abuse of Women.* Geneva, Switzerland: World Council of Churches, 2013.

Block, Heather, Kathy Shantz, Beth Graybill, Kathryn Mitchell Loewen, Judith Snowdon, Lori Matties, MCC Women's Concerns Network, Elsie Goerzen, Abuse Response and Prevention Program, MCC BC Virginia Froese, Voices for Non-Violence, MCC Manitoba Jane Woelk, Voices for Non-Violence, MCC Manitoba, Linda Gehman Peachey, Women's Advocacy Program, MCC US Dana Hepting, Graphic Designer, MCC Canada. *Understanding Sexual Abuse by a Church Leader or Caregiver, 2nd ed.* Winnipeg, CA: Mennonite Central Committee Canada, 2016. https://abuseresponseandprevention.ca/wp-content/uploads/2015/10/UnderstandingSexualAbusebyaChurchLeaderBooklet15_web.pdf.

Bodden, Richardo, *Leadership in the Age of Narcissism: God's Blueprint for Christian Leaders* Franklin, TN: Carpenter's Son Publishing, 2020.

Denhollander, Rachael, Mika Edmondson, Samantha Kilpatrick, Diane Langberg, Chris Moles, Andrea Munford, Karla Siu, Darby Strickland, and Leslie Vernick. *Becoming a Church That Cares Well for the Abused:*

Handbook. Edited by Brad Hambrick. Nashville: B&H Publishing, 2019. https://churchcares.com/assets/downloads/ChurchCares.pdf.

Fjelstad, Margalis. *Stop Caretaking the Borderline or Narcissist: How to End the Drama and Get On with Life.* London: Rowman & Littlefield, 2013.

Goodman, Cynthia Lechan, and Barbara Leff. *The Everything Guide to Narcissistic Personality Disorder: Professional, reassuring advice for coping with the disorder—at work, at home, and in your family.* Avon, MA: Adams Media, 2012.

Hunt, June. *Biblical Counseling Keys on Forgiveness.* Plano, TX: Hope for the Heart, 2014.

Keller, Tim. *Forgive: Why Should I and How Can I?* New York: Viking Press, 2022.

Kruger, Michael J. *Bully Pulpit: Confronting the Problem of Spiritual Abuse in the Church.* Grand Rapids, MI: Zondervan, 2022.

Meier, Paul D. and Robert L. Wise. *Crazy Makers: Getting Along with the Difficult People in Your Life.* Nashville: Thomas Nelson Publishers, 2003.

National Sexual Violence Resource Center. www.nsvrc.org.

Salter, Anna C. *Predators: Pedophiles, Rapists, and Other Sex Offenders.* New York: Perseus Books/Basic Books, 2003.

Sande, Ken. *Peacemaker: A Biblical Guide to Resolving Personal Conflict.* Grand Rapids: Baker Books, 2004.

Turner, Merethe Dahl. "Abusive Leadership: Preventing Abuse and Misuse of Power in Christian Ministry." Published July 2024. https://lausanne.org/global-analysis/abusive-leadership

Vieth, Victor, and Craig L. Nessan, eds. "Child Abuse and the Church: Prevention, Pastoral Care, and Healing." *Currents in Theology and Mission* 45, no. 3 (2018): 1-2. https://currentsjournal.org/index.php/currents/article/view/126/144.

Vital Church Ministry. www.vitalchurchministry.org.

Waterstradt, Carolyn. *Fighting the Good Fight: Healing and Advocacy after Clergy Sexual Assault.* Splattered Ink Press, 2012.

ACKNOWLEDGMENTS

God has ordained every step of this journey, and I acknowledge His presence and strength, first and foremost. He has never left me alone.

Second, to those who have come forward as the abused or the approached, thank you. I believe you; I value your trust; I'm sorry for what happened and how; I am proud of you, and I am grateful for your courage. While I can never fully understand what you experienced, I do have a taste of what you endured to stand up and say, "Enough."

Thank you to the professionals who helped along the way: Kip W, Eric N, Don B, Pete S, Lisa F, David T, Bill K, Scott N, and James W. Special thanks to the folks at Noble Creative Press, Believers Book Services, and Great Ridge Group.

And finally, my family: son Brad and Hannah (and grandson Pax), and daughter Leah and Zac (and grandson Theo, and our dear foster grandkids), my siblings Jim, Karen, Sue, and Jim, and my in-laws Betty, Pete, Vic, Kathy, Vince, and Annette. I also include my extended family: Sam and Kellie, and Jim and Lora. They have been such an encouragement, stood by me when I was leveled in tears or anger, and they have tolerated my "blank stare" when I was internally working through things that were before or beyond adequate words to express.

Abundant thanks to my wife Michelle, who has supported and encouraged this study, and shared efforts in ministry, offering real perspective from her own experiences and wisdom, always in love and grace. Michelle is an authentic and humble representation of God, and a blessing to me beyond words.

Truly, it takes a village. And I'm part of a good one.

ABOUT THE AUTHOR

Robert A. Damon completed studies in pastoral ministry at Minnesota Bible College in Rochester, Minnesota, and graduate studies in church leadership at Hope International University in Fullerton, California, with additional training in conflict and discipleship.

He worked in marketplace settings for more than fifteen years in various management roles, and then in full-time ministry, where he served in several settings for more than thirty years as pastor and professor.

Robert has authored several articles in the *Christian Standard*, *Leadership Journal*, *Small Groups Network*, and *Christianity Today*. In 2021, he authored a historic narrative called *The Land Tells a Story: A Short History of a Place Called Amnicon*.

Robert currently serves as a volunteer at Camp Amnicon in northern Wisconsin, adjunct professor in pastoral ministry, and mentors and encourages young leaders through prayer, encouragement, and regular contact.

Robert and Michelle enjoy spending time with their kids and grandchildren, and they frequently travel. They live in Saint Paul, Minnesota.

www.ingramcontent.com/pod-product-compliance
Lightning Source LLC
Chambersburg PA
CBHW070637030426
42337CB00020B/4046